ISLINGTON PAST

A Visual History of Islington

by
John Richardson

HISTORICAL PUBLICATIONS

First published 1988
by Historical Publications Ltd.
54 Station Road, New Barnet, Herts
and 32 Ellington Street, N7
(Telephone 01–607 1628)

ISBN 0 948667 01 X

Typeset by Historical Publications Ltd.
and Fakenham Photosetting Ltd.

Cover design by Aran Taylor

Printed in Great Britain by
Billing & Sons Ltd, Worcester

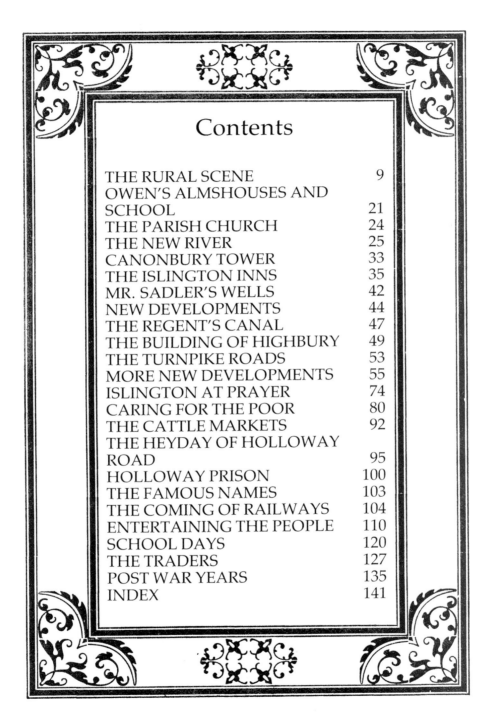

Contents

Illustrations

The following have kindly allowed the publication of illustrations:

The London Borough of Islington, Nos. 1, 4, 8, 21, 23, 25, 26, 27, 71, 72, 73, 74, 76, 80, 86, 92, 95, 98, 101, 102, 106, 109, 116, 117, 120, 125, 126, 127, 128, 129, 130, 133, 139, 142, 143, 144, 147, 151, 152, 153, 156, 157, 159.

The Greater London Record Office, Prints and Drawings: Nos. 9, 36, 55, 66, 70, 114.

The Greater London Record Office, Photographic Library: Nos. 136, 137, 138, 140.

The Guildhall Library, Prints and Drawings: Nos. 28, 37, 79, 94, 100, 103, 104, 111, 118, 121

The Royal Commission on the Historical Monuments of England, Photographic Library: 150, 154, 155, 158

The British Museum: 7

Other illustrations are from the collection of Historical Publications Ltd.

The cover illustration of Canonbury Tower *c*1800, is reproduced by kind permission of the London Borough of Islington. It is a watercolour copied from an original drawing by Paul Sandby.

Introduction

As defined today, Islington includes the former parishes of Clerkenwell and Finsbury, two areas of London which have sufficient material of their own to each warrant single volumes. This collection of illustrations, with few exceptions, concentrates on what used to be the borough of Islington before the London reshuffle of 1965.

In the twenty years after the last war Islington was regarded as a rather seedy and run-down part of inner London. It was a suburb which had a legacy of years of building neglect. The grimy terraces and squares, though pleasant architecturally, were impossible to heat, inconvenient from the general pattern of two large rooms on each floor, and woefuly deficient in sanitary facilities and kitchens. Only the general prosperity of a burgeoning middle-class population has rescued it from further decay. This is not a viewpoint which will endear itself to everyone, but, as suggested in the last section of this book, the local authorities could not have done what has been done.

This regeneration is not, of course, peculiar to Islington. Most of the London inner suburbs have been through the same process, but Islington was one of the first places in which those with money were anxious to buy in so that they might restore old houses, and many of those without money were anxious to move out to more conventional dwellings with amenities already laid on.

The increase in office space in London was providing more jobs for the incomers, whereas industry moved out and took its workers with it. Other fates conspired to encourage this social movement. The Victoria Line made Islington more accessible. The increasing cost of transport or driving in from places much further out made an unnecessary dent in pockets and time. The development of an antiques market at Camden Passage gave Islington some unexpected notoriety. The facility to knock through walls on a complete floor of most of the houses provided the large rooms beloved of the incomers. And the architecture, lovingly renovated, was pleasing to the eye. Gradually, Islington changed its character.

The visual retrospective in this book attempts to show Islington from the 18th century, when there were 900 houses, to the quite recent era before this regeneration. At this point of seediness it had become a challenge to the planners and an attraction to the conservators. The planners and the developers lost because they already had enough to swallow and by the time they were ready for more the trend was towards keeping the rest.

There are surprisingly few books on Islington, and hardly anything has been done on late 19th- and 20th-century history. The subject awaits a dedicated researcher. Also there are many illustrations which have never been published. Some of them are in this volume, together with better-known ones which could not really be excluded from any chronological story.

John Richardson

Acknowledgements

I have received much help from the staff of the Libraries Department of the London Borough of Islington, in particular from Ms Val Dawson and David Withie. They have been most courteous and helpful in supplying material for reproduction.

Further reading

The most useful recent reference book on Islington has been *Streets with a Story: The Book of Islington*, compiled by former Islington Borough Librarian, Eric A. Willats. This takes every street in the present borough of Islington and, where possible, gives derivation, building history and notes on important buildings and residents. The *Victoria County History of Middlesex, Volume VIII*, deals with Islington and Stoke Newington; it contains much new research. More modestly priced are several booklets by local residents. By Mary Cosh there is *An Historical Walk through Barnsbury*, published in 1981, and also a publication on *The New River*. By Keith Sugden is a very useful *History of Highbury*, published in 1984.

Islington by Charles Harris (1974) contained a great many Islington anecdotes, and *Islington: A History and Guide by Pieter Zwart* (1973) is a useful, if rather jumbled, basic history.

The standard early histories of Islington are *Walks Through Islington* by Thomas Cromwell (1835), *History and Topography . . . of St. Mary's Islington*, by Samuel Lewis (1842), *History, Topography and Antiquities of . . . St. Mary's, Islington*, by John Nelson (1823), and *Yseldon: A Perambulation of Islington*, by Thomas Tomlins (1861). There is also much of Islington interest in *The History of Clerkenwell* by W. J. Pinks (1865).

1. *A Bird's Eye View of Islington from Canonbury Tower.* Published in 1835, but probably based on an earlier drawing. In the centre may be seen St. Paul's Cathedral and, to the right, the spire of St Mary's, Islington.

The Rural Scene

It is difficult, even with the help of those contemporary views which exist, to envisage a rural Islington, or indeed the extent of the open country around the cities of London and Westminster in the 18th century. Only when you cycle are you made aware of the considerable number of hills in Islington, now disguised by the street landscape and the comfort of driving. *The Bird's Eye View* above, published in 1835, but probably based on a slightly earlier perspective, shows the open fields between Canonbury Tower and St. Mary's church, bisected by the winding New River. That particular curve of this artificial stream is a popular centrepiece of a number of rural Islington views – it is still above ground and picturesque at this point off Canonbury Road today. With its open country and pleasant streams Islington was regarded as a place for city people to go for a day out, but it was probably no more favoured in this respect than other villages within walking distance – Kentish Town, Hackney and Kensington are extolled for the same reason.

At Islington the roads from London, today's St. John Street and Goswell Road, branched north and east. Via Upper Street and Holloway Road the traveller went north, or else he went east along the Lower Road, (today's Essex Road), to Hackney and Essex. Along these two roads herds of cattle went to Smithfield for sale or slaughter. In 1754 the number passing through the Islington turnpike, at the junction with Liverpool Road, was nearly 29,000 oxen and 267,000 sheep, not to mention other beasts. The sheer weight of them, all milling around before the tollgate, may have been responsible for the fact that the roadway is now much lower than the pavement at this point, or else the pavement was built up to avoid their mire.

In 1756 the New Road by-pass around north London was begun. This route, today's Marylebone, Euston and Pentonville Roads, went through open country and avoided parish centres except that of Islington. And then, five years later, the City Road was added so that the traveller could reach Finsbury Square and the City in some comfort. Islington was firmly on the map.

This meeting of the roads brought an end to Islington's tranquility. A map of 1735, *(Illustration 3)*, shows the area before this transformation, although its emptiness disguises the existence of over 900 houses in the parish at the time. Today's principal roads are there – Upper Street and Essex Road are fairly well inhabited, with the 'Cross' Street already built up, but the Back Road, now Liverpool Road, is merely a short cut through the fields to Ring Cross on the Holloway Road, an area regarded as beyond respectability and hence the site of the local gibbet and first workhouse. On the Back Road there were many lairs for the cattle on their way to Smithfield; the animals were left here overnight while the drovers stayed locally, and then taken down St. John Street the next day. The small paths connecting Upper Street and the Back Road are on the line of present roads. Hopping Lane is the present St. Paul's/Ball's Pond Road with an offshoot, roughly on the line of Highbury Park, northwards to Cream Hall at Stroud Green. To the west an important road, now York Way/Brecknock Road, marks the boundary between Islington and St. Pancras parishes, here shown deserted apart from the oddly situated and named Copenhagen House *(Illustrations 11 & 12)*.

Larger houses included Canonbury Tower and a building described as Highbury, but which was really the inn and tea gardens called Highbury Barn. To the west of this was Jack Straw's Castle, denoting the site of the Highbury manor house, a building virtually destroyed in 1381 by Jack Straw's followers in the Peasants' Revolt against the Poll Tax of the day. This site, approximately that of Leigh Road today, has more justification for association with Jack Straw than does the famous public house in Hampstead.

Islington Green included almshouses, a watch-house at its apex, a cage for the temporary imprisonment of wrongdoers, a pound for the containment of stray cattle, and a maypole. The Green fell into disrepute and was used as a dung-heap until the lord of the manor of Canonbury, the Marquess of Northampton, granted the ground to the vestry in 1777, and it was cleared and fenced off.

Along Upper Street the 15th-century parish church of St. Mary is shown but not marked. At the time this church had authority throughout the whole area of Islington. Church of England worshippers in such outlying settlements as Upper Holloway, Newington and Kingsland would have been obliged to attend St Mary's at least once a month for Holy Communion but may well have used closer chapels such as the ones at Highgate and Kingsland on other Sundays.

2. Islington in 1780. This view, published in *Old and New London*, (c1873), was probably copied from an earlier print. It shows the pound on Islington Green with, it seems, right-of-way for carts and carriages to cross from Essex Road up the slope to Upper Street. St. Mary's is in the background.

Facing page:
3. A Survey of the Roads and Foot-paths in the Parish of Islington. From a Plan in the Vestry Room. Drawn in the Year 1735. This is the earliest parish map of Islington.

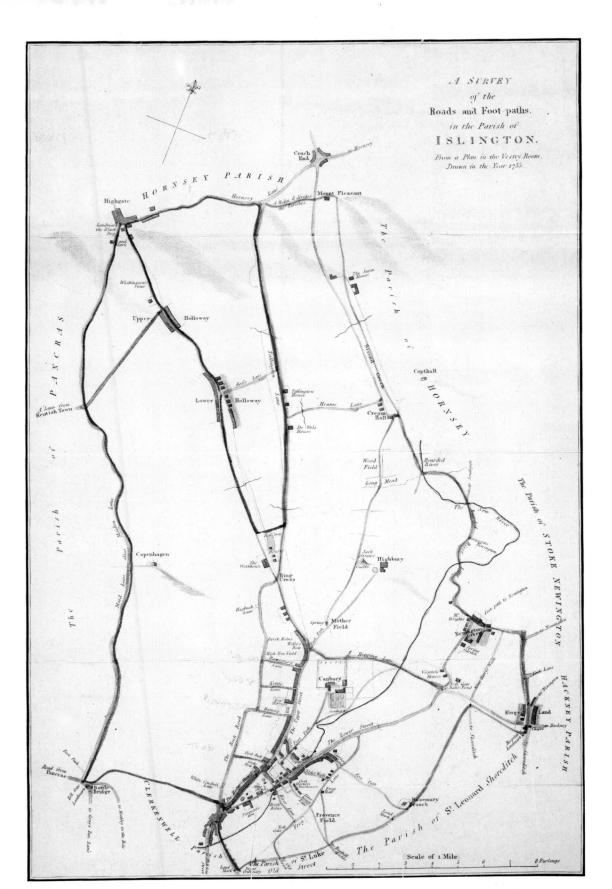

A SURVEY
of the
Roads and Foot-paths.
in the Parish of
ISLINGTON.
From a Plan in the Vestry Room.
Drawn in the Year 1735.

HORNSEY PARISH

Cruch End
to Hornsey

Highgate
Hornsey Lane
A Beam divides the Parishes
Mount Pleasant

Landmark the Black Dog
Land Mark

The Japan House

Whittington's Stone

Upper Holloway

Strout Green

Copthall

The Parish of HORNSEY

Roffe Lane

Tollington House

Tollington Lane

Lower Holloway
Heame Lane

De Vols House
Cream Hall

A Lane from Kentish Town

Muken Lane

Wood Field

Boarded River

Long Mead

The Parish of PANCRAS

Maid Lane alias

Copenhagen

Halfway House

The Workhouse

Ring Cross

Jack Straws Castle

Highbury

The New River

foot path to Newington

to Newington

The Parish of STOKE NEWINGTON

Hagbush Lane

Spring Mother Field

Brick Kilns
Wells Row

High Tree Field

Kettle Lane

Battery Lane

Canbury

Hopping Lane

Mr Wrights

Newington Green

Cyrian Garden

Virginia House

Toll gate
to Ball's Pond
Newington Road Walk

Cock Lane

to Newington

HACKNEY PARISH

Kings Land

Land

to Hackney

Road from Pancras
Foot Path

The Lower Street
to Shoreditch

to Shoreditch

Chapel

Battle Bridge

Toll Gate
Landmark

The Rush Road

The Upper Street

Ford Path

Ford Pull

Rosemary Branch

to Gray's Inn Lane
to Bexley in the Vale

CLERKENWELL

White Conduit Lane

Baker Well Lane

Frog Lane

Foot Path

to Shoreditch

Hoxton Landmark

Provence Field

The Parish of St Leonard Shoreditch

Pyeposts Row

Brick Kilns

Toll Gate

Fitzfield

Land Mark

Parish

The Parish of St Luke Old Street

Land Mark
Day of Ordinary

Scale of 1 Mile
2   3   4   5   6   7   8 Furlongs

4. *A Duel in Islington Fields.* An 18th-century view.

Duelling became not just fashionable, but an obsession, in the 18th century. Though not formally prohibited until 1818 it was regarded as an offence long before then and, consequently, contestants in this formalised murder tended to use unfrequented places in which to uphold their perceived honour. Places like Chalk Farm, Putney, Kensington and Islington were regarded as suitable venues. The authorities seldom acted unless a fatality occurred, but the survivor was usually dealt with lightly, a consequence of a romantic conception of chivalry and a regard for the usual social class of the participants.

It is often suggested that the last stylised, formal (and fatal) duel in England took place near the Brecknock Tavern on 1 July 1843, in the fields on either the Islington or St. Pancras side of the road. A Lt. Colonel Fawcett was shot by his brother-in-law, a fellow soldier. The wounded man, refused admission to the Tavern, was taken to a public house in Camden Town, where he died. In this case a verdict of murder was returned at the inquest but in the event the survivor was acquitted.

John Nelson, author of *The History and Antiquities of Islington* (1823), refers to a duel at Islington in 1609 in which both contestants, one a godson of the king, were killed; they were buried in the same grave.

5. *South view of White Conduit House, 1731.* From the *History of Clerkenwell* by W.J. Pinks, *(1865)*.

At the bottom of today's Barnsbury Road, near the junction with Maygood Street, was a spring from which water was fed by conduit to Charterhouse as early as 1431. From this simple beginning developed one of Islington's 18th-century attractions, though strictly speaking the Conduit was just outside the Islington boundary at the time, in Clerkenwell. A tavern was built to exploit the none-too-plentiful water; this opened, it is said, the very day in 1649 on which Charles I was executed. By the time the 18th-century obsession for spas, wells and waters reached its peak the White Conduit House had become more a tea garden attraction, for it is doubtful if the depleted spring rivalled the wells around King's Cross or that at Hampstead or that, indeed, at nearby Sadler's Wells.

The White Conduit House was enlarged in 1754 when the proprietor advertised a new Long Walk, a fish pond, a 'number of shady pleasant arbours' and privacy from onlookers. He also promised hot loaves and fresh milk and butter and, indeed, White Conduit loaves were a familiar item to Londoners. There was competition in Penton Street from Dobney's Tea Gardens and bowling green and from the Belvedere at the corner with the New Road, which earlier had been called Busby's Folly.

Goldsmith visited the White Conduit House after dinners at Highbury Barn and for a while the place had a reputation for discreet indecorum, but during the height of its popularity in the early 1820s it became rowdier. In 1828 it was rebuilt on a grander scale but, as with similar places in London, its time had come. Despite increasingly elaborate entertainments in the way of music, dancing, trade dinners and the like, its clientèle dwindled just as the area itself was beginning to be built up. Its extensive grounds were too valuable as building land and the old tavern was demolished in 1849, to be superseded by a smaller building.

The White Conduit House did, though, have a place in trade union history. It was here, in 1836, that an illustrious dinner was held to celebrate the success of a public campaign to cut short the sentences of transportation on the Tolpuddle Martyrs. The evening was presided over by Thomas Wakley, editor of *The Lancet* and its function was described as 'in Com-

6. *White Conduit House, about 1820.* From *Old and New London*.

memoration of the Moral Power displayed by the Working Classes of London in their great procession of April 1834'. This described a well-attended march of trade-unionists, two years earlier, from Copenhagen Fields to Whitehall to plead the Dorset labourers' cause. These events have been marked recently by naming the new road near the site of the Conduit, Tolpuddle Street.

By the time the House was demolished the actual spring had long been unused. In 1810 a lay preacher called William Huntington dredged it so that it might be used again by local inhabitants, but his religious views were so disliked that vandals promptly fouled the spring with filth again. This thwarted enterprise appears to mark the last time the spring was of consequence.

The White House fields were much used for recreation such as archery and cricket. *Illustration 8* depicts a cricket game in 1784 whose details have survived, when the teams included some members of the peerage. Matches on this site led to the forma-

tion of the Marylebone Cricket Club – the MCC. Former members of the White Conduit Club began the MCC in 1787 when they played their former Islington colleagues at a site in Marylebone (now covered by Dorset Square) leased from Thomas Lord; the two clubs were later merged.

7. Islington from the New River. An illustration by George Scharf, *(1788–1860),* dated 1816. It is the first London drawing by this artist. The view looks towards St. Mary's Islington, and the artist is in today's Douglas Road just below Willow Bridge Road.

George Scharf, the artist of this illustration, was born in Bavaria in 1788. He came to London in 1816 and this view of Islington is the first of his London drawings. The viewpoint can be readily identified today as by the New River Walk, the artist seated in what would now be a front garden in Douglas Road, with Willow Bridge Road in the bottom right corner. St. Mary's, Islington, may be seen in the centre and St. Paul's Cathedral to the left. It is remarkable to think that you could be at ground level and see the dome of St. Paul's almost without interruption. Nowadays, not only houses impede the view, but also trees which are remarkably absent from the Scharf landscape.

The building with the portico to the right of the picture may be the old Canonbury Tavern in Canonbury Lane and the building to its left partly hidden by trees is, presumably, Canonbury Tower.

Scharf went on to record much of inner London and his work, which has great charm, is an invaluable reference to the buildings of the day. He was, as well, at hand to draw the ruins of the Houses of Parliament when they were destroyed by fire in 1834, and also the demolition of a sizeable area of the City when the new London Bridge was built. Not that his talent brought him much money. On the contrary, he died a very poor man, dependent on charity, in 1860. One of his sons became Secretary to the newly-formed National Portrait Gallery.

The map of 1735 shows parts of Upper Street and Essex Road already developed, together with Cross Street and a few lesser roads around the Green. Thirty years later a terrace of houses appeared in what became Liverpool Road, called Paradise Row, raised quite high above the road. Much of this terrace (numbers 495–507) survives today and its name is derived from Paradise House, a mansion near the Mackenzie Road end. A decade later, about 1773, Henry Penton, MP for Winchester, began to lay out roads on his estate north of the New Road, and on this he built Pentonville, one of London's first planned suburbs.

Highbury was the next area of consequence to be developed: this is dealt with on p49. Barnsbury was built from the 1820s. It included Reedmoat Field, shown in *Illustration 9*, the site of Barnsbury Square. The moat once surrounded a medieval house, but has long since been thought to indicate a Roman settlement. This house was held by the Berners fami-

ly, from whom Barnsbury derives its name. Barnsbury was developed in terraces and squares but presumably, as there are few mews properties, the developers had in mind people too poor to afford their own carriages but rich enough to pay several servants. From here it was possible to walk to work in the City, and from the Angel there were numerous coaches.

The principal estates within Barnsbury were those of Cloudesley, Milner-Gibson, Thornhill and the Drapers' Company.

The development of the area was fortuitous for at least one local firm – Dove Brothers, the builders, who still exist today. They had a hand in much Islington building and many north London churches. Cloudesley Square was first occupied in 1826 and the church necessary to keep up the tone and the value of the area opened soon after in its centre. Thomas Milner-Gibson of Theberton Hall, Suffolk, de-

8. Cricket. Played by the Gentlemen's Club. White Conduit House. 1784.

veloped Gibson Square in the 1830s and Milner Square a decade later. The latter is, architecturally, one of the most unusual squares in London. Until its recent renovation and cleansing by Islington Council, it was reviled as being grim and without grace. However, its present pristine state shows that the architects, Alexander Dick and Robert Roumieu, built it with much elegance. Thornhill Road and Square spanned the 1820s–40s, the latter more an ellipse than a square, and Lonsdale Square *(Illustration 70)*, built on Gosseyfield in the 1840s, completed the principal elements of Barnsbury development.

Simultaneously the Canonbury Estate was being developed, but on grander lines and with the emphasis on semi-detached villas rather than on terraces. Its principal feature, Canonbury Square, was first occupied in 1826, (the same year as Cloudesley Square), but its harmony has been rudely shattered by the traffic flow through it. The Square's architect was Henry Leroux, who had also designed Compton Terrace twenty years earlier. In fact, this period was

quite a significant one in Islington building history, for, apart from the developments mentioned above, two striking buildings were erected in isolated pockets of the parish. Right in the north, flanking the new Archway Road, the Company of Mercers rebuilt in 1822 the almshouses founded by the 15th-century bequest of Richard Whittington, popular Lord Mayor of London, and in Highbury, the Highbury College was built for the training of Dissenting clergy. The grounds of the latter building, *(Illustration 59)*, were later absorbed by the Arsenal Football Club.

Within the space of about thirty years, the fields of inner Islington disappeared and this area, at least, of the parish became part of the burgeoning metropolis.

9. *Reedmoat Field*. An early 19th-century view of the site of a moated farmhouse on which stands today's Barnsbury Square. The view appears to be towards the north-west, showing Copenhagen House in the centre and the hills of Hampstead and Highgate in the distance.

Facing page:
10. *Ancient Houses in Islington High Street.*

Facing page:
11. *Old Copenhagen House.* Mid 18th-century view of house before it became a fashionable venue.

There is no satisfactory explanation for the name of Copenhagen House. It was known as such by 1695 and may well derive from the marriage of James I to Anne of Denmark; it is also suggested, but without proof, that the house was occupied by the Danish ambassador during the Great Plague. It was a place of public entertainment by the 1750s, with the obligatory tea gardens on a site overlooking London. Later, its premises were used for bull-baiting and it lost its licence in 1816. A subsequent owner was a firm supporter of the radical group, The London Corresponding Society, and a number of large pro-revolutionary meetings were held in the grounds of the house. Its last significant gathering was one addressed by Louis Kossuth, the Hungarian patriot, in 1851.

The house and its grounds were chosen by the Corporation of London as the site for a new cattle market to replace Smithfield, leaving the latter just to deal with carcasses. The whole area, including both sides of Market Road, now occupied by local authority housing, playing fields and gardens, was taken up by pens, administrative buildings and a clock-tower of much elegance built on the site of the old house.

12. *Copenhagen House.* The house at the beginning of the 19th century, at the height of its prosperity.

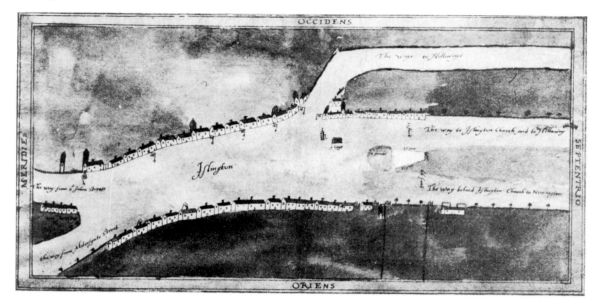

13. *A Plan of Islington in Tudor times.*

The village centre of Islington was very close to the parish border, so close that part of the High Street was in the parish of Clerkenwell. In modern times Clerkenwell was absorbed by Finsbury and, in its turn, the latter has become part of Islington. Two early ventures, both close by in Clerkenwell, the Dame Alice Owen Almshouses and School, and the New River Company, are inseparable from any history of Islington. These are dealt with on following pages.

Above is featured a plan of Islington drawn up sometime in the 16th century. The numerous poles with signs probably indicate inns and taverns. On the far left is what became the Angel and there are a further six drinking places up to the Liverpool Road ('The Waye to Hollo017 Waye'), and two more on the other side of the road. Just in front of the Green are some of the elements of village life at the time – the pump, the cage, and the pound. No doubt it was on this Green that the four Islington Protestant martyrs were burnt in 1557 during the Marian repression.

14. *The Old Almshouses of Lady Owen.* From *The History of Clerkenwell* by W.J. Pinks, (1865).

Owen's Almshouses and School

15. *The Second Almshouses of Lady Owen.*

16. *The Old Grammar School of Lady Owen*. From *The History of Clerkenwell* by W.J. Pinks, *(1865)*.

The traditional story as to the founding of Dame Alice Owen's almshouses and school is that when she was young she escaped death when a stray arrow from the archery butts in fields near Islington, pierced her hat but missed her head. This encouraged a vow that if she lived to be a lady she would erect a building on the site which would give thanks for and commemorate her deliverance. This long-broadcast story may well be true, although there is not even an oblique reference to the incident in the Letters Patent granted for her scheme in 1608. She was, by all accounts, a charitable woman and the setting up of almshouses and a free school were conventional ways of appeasing the fates at the end of one's life. Alice, herself the daughter of an Islington landholder whose name appears in the 16th-century Islington parish registers, married three times, lastly to Thomas Owen, a Justice of the Common Pleas and himself a philanthropist; he died in 1598 leaving her rich enough to carry out her pledge. She purchased the Hermitage fields at the junction of

St. John Street and Goswell Road, and by 1611 the almshouses for ten widows shown in *Illustration 14* had been built. She then made a new application to the Crown to establish the school and this was built by 1613 *(Illustration 16)*. To secure the administration of these two projects in perpetuity she vested them in a City livery company – the Brewers', a common device since, apart from the Church, no other suitable bodies existed.

Rebuilding took place 1840/1 to the designs of George Tattersall, architect to the Brewers. He allowed the pupils three schoolrooms, a desk apiece with twenty-two inches of space, but no playground. These scholars, (boys only), were selected from the poor of both Clerkenwell and Islington as, indeed, were the widows in the almshouses, who had to be at least fifty years of age. In 1886 a girls' school was added in Owen's Row, necessitating the demolition of the almshouses. Some of these buildings were destroyed in the last war and the schools now continue at Potters Bar.

17. *The second Grammar School of Lady Owen,* from *The History of Clerkenwell,* by W.J. Pinks, *(1865).*

18. *Old St. Mary's church, Islington.* The building was demolished in 1751.

The Parish Church

St. Mary's church in Upper Street has had a number of predecessors. There was a building here in the 12th century, and a new one, shown in *Illustration 18*, was built in the 15th century. When demolition of this building took place in 1751 a date, 1483, was found engraved on the old steeple and this could be the exact year of this structure. The tower and spire which are there today are part of the church which opened in 1754, designed by a joiner called Launcelot Dowbiggin who, it is said, made the style of the spire from a combination of his favourite London churches. Thirty years later his spire was in some danger of collapse and an ingenious contraption of wicker, shaped like a beehive, was erected around it in place of scaffolding, from which workmen could restore the building. This tourist attraction of the time, made mostly of willow and hazel, contained an interior spiral staircase which wound around the spire. It is reported that the creator of this early piece of plant hire made more money from sightseers than from the actual commission to repair the spire.

In September 1940 the bulk of the church, except the tower and spire, was destroyed in bombing. It

19. *St. Mary's church, Islington.* Erected 1754.

20. *Sir Hugh Myddelton, promoter of the New River scheme.*

was rebuilt and finished in 1956.

The churchyard has contained surprisingly few illustrious names. Dowbiggin himself was buried here; Richard Cloudesley, who gave an estate to the parish in the 16th century and is now best known for the Square named after him, lies in a vault, and the tomb of Dame Alice Owen was transferred to the new church when it was built in 1754. In 1790 a 'John-Hyacinth Magelhaens' was buried here without tombstone; he was a great-grandson of the famous navigator.

Until the early part of the 19th century St. Mary's served the whole parish, but the Rev Daniel Wilson, appointed vicar of Islington in 1824, energetically set out to increase the number of parish churches in Islington.

The New River

Sir Hugh Myddelton, (c1560–1631), son of a Member of Parliament, was sent up to London from his native Wales to train as a goldsmith. His talents took him into banking and other speculations, one of which was to earn him the regard of generations of Londoners. Confronted with the ever worsening state of London's water supply, the City Corporation had already received permission to exploit the waters of the Hertfordshire rivers of Chadwell and Amwell, but had done nothing, and it was Sir Hugh who took on the financing, the difficult negotiations with landholders, and also the general supervision of the building of the New River. Myddelton himself was impoverished by the scheme; at a crucial point during construction it was the King rather than the

21. *An 18th-century view of the New River Head, showing the engine house.*

S. View of the New River Head.

22. *A 17th-century view of the New River Head.*

City who came to his financial aid to ensure comple-
tion, despite Myddelton's excellent connections in
the City. Needless to say, the Lord Mayor was happy
to be present to open the New River in 1613.

The New River was a canal approximately 10ft
wide and 4ft deep, winding about 39 miles from the
rivers of Chadwell and Amwell near Ware to a reservoir called the New River Head off Amwell Street in
Clerkenwell. From this point it was distributed by
wooden pipes to various City destinations. The idea
for the River was not Myddelton's. Something similar was suggested earlier by a Captain Edmund
Colthurst who applied for Letters Patent to carry out
the work. The City, unhappy that a private individual might do what they themselves had neglected, quickly obtained their own Bill, compensated
Colthurst and then did nothing, whereupon Colthurst renewed his scheme and the permission to the
City was transferred to the Captain. One of his part-
ners was Sir Hugh Myddelton, known to City digni-
taries, and it was to him that the Corporation transferred its licences, and it was Myddelton who became the figurehead of the venture.

The original intention was to complete within four
years and, in the event, despite many hindrances
and unfamiliar problems to solve, this target was
nearly met. Survey work began in March 1609 and by
September 130 labourers were engaged in the work.
The first, and most serious hurdle was an unexpected
grouping of landowners who tried to get the Bill
repealed, a threat only removed when Parliament
was dissolved, leaving Myddelton free to proceed.
The scheme ran into financial difficulties and it was
King James I who offered to pay half the expendi-
ture, past and future, in exchange for half the profits.
With the King's backing there was no further trouble
with the landlords when work restarted in Novem-
ber 1611, and within two years the rest of the canal
was cut. The grand opening at New River Head was
on September 29th, 1613.

More difficult than the task of bringing the water to
the borders of Islington was that of distributing it to
City households. The wooden pipes, shown in *Illustration 25*, were made of elm, quite often bored out by
horse-driven augers and then tapered to interlock;
the usual life-span of a pipe was about 4–7 years, and

Facing page:
23. *By the waterhouse of the New River.*

Facing page:
24. *The New River Head*, at the beginning of the 18th century.

so there was constant maintenance. The first line went to St. John Street, Smithfield and Newgate, where it branched to Cheapside and Ludgate. The scheme was not an encouraging success. In the first place the wooden pipes could not contain very high pressure and therefore only ground floor premises could be supplied. Secondly the supply was by no means constant. There was also a popularly-held antagonism to water carried in pipes as opposed to that coming fresh out of contaminated local wells. Even by 1618 there were only 1000 customers, but by 1622 the venture was just in profit. Charles I, who sold his shares in 1631, in despair of making much out of them, was not to know that early in the 20th century just one share would sell at auction for £125,000.

Later improvements included a windmill erected near the New River Head in 1709 to pump water to a new reservoir in today's Claremont Square, the water in this being used to supply houses on higher ground. Thirty years later permission was received to take water from the River Lea to cope with the increased demand. The next major improvement in the scheme occurred from 1812 when iron pipes were introduced.

25. *The wooden pipes of the New River.*

26. *Constructing a New River pipeline.*

The Company's surveyor until he died in 1811 was Robert Mylne. He was succeeded by his son, William Chadwick Mylne, who laid out the estate on the Company's land – by him were built Myddelton Square, Claremont Square and Amwell Street, and also the church of St. Mark.

When the New River Company was absorbed at the beginning of this century by the Metropolitan Water Board, the New River Head was drained and the headquarters of the Board built on the site. Gradually the mechanics of water production were pushed further north so that all that was left in Islington was the ornamental walk off Canonbury Road. The New River still supplies much of north London's water but a new deep mains being constructed will make the old canal redundant by 1990.

Artists who have depicted the New River include Wenceslaus Hollar, (1607–1677), a popular illustrator of 17th-century London, and Thomas Hosmer Shepherd, who was very much an Islington resident. He was born in France but within six weeks he was christened in St. Luke's, Old Street; his father, George, also an artist, settled the family off the City Road. By 1820 Thomas was, with his own young family, at 26 Chapman (now Batchelor) Street, Islington, which still survives, and where they remained until 1842. Shepherd became the foremost topographical artist of his day, his main achievement being the 159 illustrations used in a book called *Metropolitan Improvements*, which depicted the principal new London buildings of the early 19th century. Shepherd's subsequent Islington homes were in Colebrook Row, Reid Street and 5 Cloudesley Square, where he died.

27. *Construction of the New River reservoir at Claremont Square*. To the left is the continuation of Amwell Street and in the background is Pentonville Road with the Belvedere tavern at the corner of Penton Street.

28. *Canonbury Tower in the 17th century.*

Canonbury Tower

Canonbury Tower, one of the oldest surviving buildings in Islington, has an even longer history. In 1253 the estate in which it stands was given by the Berners family to the Canons of St Bartholomew's Priory in London, and it became known as the Canons' burgh, corrupted later to the manor of Canonbury. A substantial manor house was erected by William Bolton, prior from 1509 to 1532, probably on the site of an older structure. This fell victim to the Crown at the Dissolution and went into the ample pocket of Thomas Cromwell, who appears to have been already living here from 1533. Substantial rebuilding occurred during the ownership in the 1590s of the enormously rich Lord Mayor of London, Sir John Spencer; the tower and a long first-floor gallery date from his time. In the 19th century the tower is recorded as having seven stories and twenty-three rooms, let out as lodgings. The Spencer family names of Compton and Alwyne are liberally scattered in the area. A south range was added in the early 18th century, and by then the house was more a cluster of buildings let separately. Residents of various parts have included Sir Francis Bacon, Oliver Goldsmith, Ephraim Chambers, the founder of the Encyclopaedia bearing his name and, briefly, Washington Irving, the American writer who created Rip Van Winkle.

The tower was restored by the Marquess of Northampton, descendant of Sir John Spencer, in 1907. The King Edward Hall was built for the recreation of his tenants and this was converted into the Tower Theatre in 1952 by the Tavistock Repertory Theatre, an amateur company which had moved from the Mary Ward Settlement in Tavistock Place, Bloomsbury.

Facing page:
29. *Canonbury Tower*, a view published in 1846.

30. *The Mail Coach at the Angel, Islington, on the Night of His Majesty's Birthday*. A coloured aquatint by James Pollard, (1812).

The Islington Inns

A general observation about Islington is that all the pubs are on one side of the road and the buildings which signify authority and good intentions are on the other. This is not strictly true, but if you look along Islington High Street and Upper Street there are numerous pubs on the left, and on the right you have the Green which previously held the lock-up and pound, and in Upper Street you have three churches, a town hall, and a police and fire station. Furthermore, most of the principal places of entertainment have been or are on the public-house side.

For reasons mentioned earlier Islington was an important stage on the route to the City or Smithfield. People coming from the north would either reach Highgate and stay there before the final part of the journey, hence the number of inns in *that* village, or else they would get as far as Islington with its convenient fields and lairs for cattle.

The two most important inns in coaching days were the Angel and the Peacock, both of which no longer trade. The use of the name 'Angel' for an inn is very ancient and an inn here in the fifteenth century is more than possible. The Tudor or 17th-century version, pictured in *Illustrations 30 and 31*, was demolished in 1819; its successor was rebuilt in 1880, the splendid cupola being added in 1899 in the prosperous times when trade was good from the number of visitors to the Royal Agricultural Hall. It was a Lyons Corner House from 1921–1959, then served as an annexe to the City University and is now a bank. As *Illustration 31* shows, the old inn had a yard with double galleries; in the quadrangle occasional dramatic or musical performances were given. James Pollard's aquatint of 1812, (*Illustration 30*), shows us the frontage a few years before its demolition. Another well-known scene by Pollard, who was born in what is now known as Exmouth Street, is of the north-country mails arriving at the Peacock at No. 11 Islington High Street. This closed as a public house in 1962, although much of the frontage depicted by Pollard survives.

The most frequently pictured of the Islington inns was the Old Queen's Head at No. 44 Essex Road. No date is known for its building but presumably it was at least as old as the 16th century. Sadly, it was demolished in 1829. Ten years later another picturesque structure went – The Three Hats near the corner with Liverpool Road; a fire that destroyed two adjoining houses damaged the roof of the inn so badly that it had to be demolished. Like Dobney's Pleasure Gardens at the bottom of Penton Street, it had a reputation for equestrian entertainments in its back field.

The old Highbury Brewery is shown in *Illustration 36*. This building on Holloway Road has been demolished, but to the left of it may be seen its retail outlet, the Highbury Tap, which still exists today, and which has in recent times, with the renewed interest in good beer, enlarged its brewing activities. The brewery began *c*1814 out of the activities at Highbury Barn, where the demand for beer was so large that the brewery there could not cope. William Willoughby, the proprietor of the Barn, built a new brewery in the Holloway Road to supply his own and other establishments.

31. *The Angel Inn Yard*, an engraving published in 1819.

32. *The Angel Inn*, a postcard *c*1905.

33. *The Old Queen's Head, Essex Road*. A view published in 1819.

34. *Canonbury Tavern, Canonbury Place*. A view published in 1819.

Highbury Barn began as just that – a farm building; by *c*1740 cakes and ale were being sold, and then it developed into a pleasure resort and tea garden; as the fashion for such places became more pronounced, a bowling green and trap-ball ground were added. Almost all pleasure resorts of the 18th century seem to have become rowdier and disreputable in the 19th century. Highbury Barn was no exception. Its last owner, Edward Giovanelli, established a new music-hall, brought on acts such as tightrope walkers, including Blondin, and a lot of drunken behaviour was reported. Perhaps the neighbours, settled in their new houses, were less tolerant, more 'Victorian' in their view of people having a good time, but in any case, opposition to the renewal of Giovanelli's licence became more concerted and in 1870 was successful. An attempt by a new licensee failed to keep it open and by 1872 the place was finally closed.

The same year that the Old Queen's Head in Essex Road was demolished another loss was incurred: the Thatched House, *(Illustration 39)*, was destroyed by fire. This building, at No. 119 Essex Road, had itself replaced a Tudor inn.

At the corner of Theberton Street and Upper Street stood the Old Pied Bull, usually reputed to have been the home, temporary residence or the property of Sir Walter Raleigh. In 1624 it was the residence of Sir John Miller, and by 1725 it had become the Pied Bull Inn and part of the Milner-Gibson estate. It was demolished in 1830.

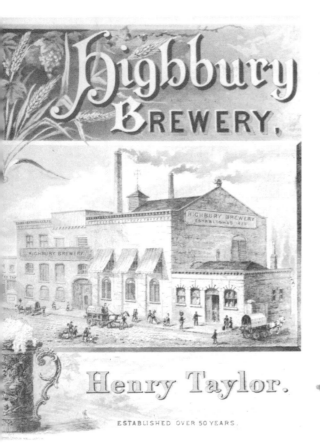

Facing page:
35. *The Three Hats, Islington.*

Top left:
36. *Highbury Brewery, Holloway Road.*

Bottom left:
37. *Highbury Barn Tea Gardens.*

Top right:
38. *Highbury Barn.* A view published in 1819.

39. *The Thatched House, Islington*. A view published in 1819.

40. *The Old Pied Bull*. A view published in 1819.

41. *Sir Walter Raleigh*.

42. *The Old Pied Bull, second building.* From a watercolour by Thomas Hosmer Shepherd.

43. *The Nag's Head, Holloway Road..* From a postcard *c*1905.

Mr. Sadler's Wells

To boost the popularity of his medicinal well Thomas Sadler built a 'musick house' in 1683. The spa declined and increasingly the building was used for entertainments of a miscellaneous and occasionally coarse nature. In 1746 Thomas Rosoman, a local builder, took over the theatre and after reviving its reputation rebuilt it in 1765. It was in this building that the famous clown, Joseph Grimaldi, first appeared as a child dancer, and Edmund Kean, as a boy, declaimed here, but because of the legal monopoly of Covent Garden and Drury Lane in the presentation of drama, the entertainments were those of variety and circus, rather than theatre. When the law was changed Samuel Phelps, actor-manager, produced thirty-four Shakespeare plays in the period of 1844–62, but it was not a success and the building was then

44. *South View of the original Sadler's Wells, 1730.* From *The History of Clerkenwell* by W.J. Pinks, *(1865)*.

45. *View of Sadler's Wells Theatre.* From *Londonia Illustrata* by Robert Wilkinson, *(1819)*.

let out for a skating rink and a boxing ring. It closed in 1878, reopened the following year for melodrama, became a music hall and then closed again in 1906.

Its subsequent career has contributed much to the English stage. The indefatigable Lilian Baylis, with Sir Reginald Rowe, raised funds to build the present theatre, designed by F.G.M. Chancellor, which opened in 1931. Since then it has been famous for opera and ballet, but its successful innovations have always moved to more central locations. Its ballet company moved to Covent Garden in 1946 to become the Royal Ballet, and in 1968 its opera company moved to the Coliseum.

46. *Spinacuti's Monkey at Sadler's Wells*, a depiction of its tricks in 1768.

47. *Sadler's Wells.* An engraving published in 1819.

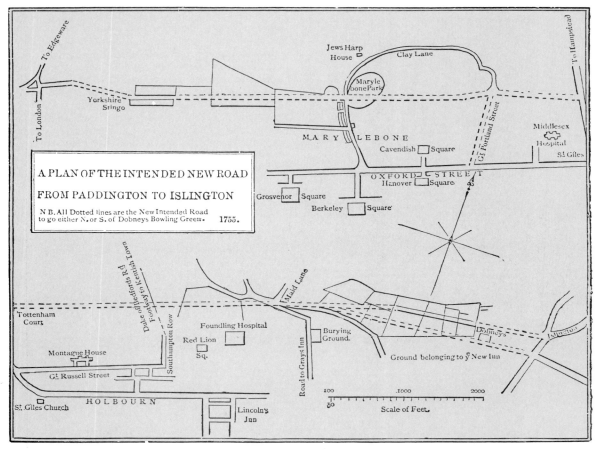

A PLAN OF THE INTENDED NEW ROAD

FROM PADDINGTON TO ISLINGTON

N B. All Dotted lines are the New Intended Road to go either N. or S. of Dobneys Bowling Green. 1755.

48. *A Plan of the Intended New Road from Paddington to Islington,* published in 1755.

New Developments

The New Road, today's Marylebone, Euston and Pentonville Roads, was London's first by-pass. Sanctioned by Parliament in 1756, it was enacted that no new buildings should be closer than fifty feet of the road; this encouraged the initial development of a *residential* road, with long front gardens of the sort still to be seen in the stretch from the top of Pentonville Hill to the Angel corner. In Parliament the proposal brought confrontation between two peers with local estates. The Duke of Bedford thought that the road, (half a mile from his house in Bloomsbury), would throw up dust to annoy him, and the Duke of Grafton, who had development sites contiguous to the proposed route, was very much in favour. The benefits of the route were clear enough to most. It meant that people travelling from the west to the City, (in particular those with herds of cattle), did not need to go through the congested and badly maintained roads of central London. With an eye to the patriotic vote, the preamble to the Act suggested that

49. *St James's church, Pentonville.*

50. *Thomas Carlyle,* from a drawing by Walter Greaves.

in times of invasion the route would provide an open road for troop movements to Essex, the most likely point of any landing. The first stretch to be opened, in the same year as the Act, was from Islington to King's Cross. The road spawned development, of course. Somers Town and Pentonville were both gambles on its popularity and neither was successful. The most important aspect of the road in London's development was that it assumed the rôle of London's northern boundary, so that when the railways threatened to intrude into the metropolis it was thought proper, at least in the north, to stop the infernal machines at the New Road. This is why the stations, Paddington, Marylebone, Euston, St. Pancras and King's Cross, are on the same line of road.

About 1773 the landowner Harry Penton laid out the first planned London suburb on both sides of the New Road. St James, Pentonville, designed by Aaron Hurst in 1787, began life as an independent chapel; two years later the parish of Clerkenwell was persuaded to take it under its wing and it became a chapel-of-ease for the residents of Pentonville un-

51. *Claremont Chapel, Pentonville Road.*

52. *John Stuart Mill,* from an oil painting by G.F.Watts, 1874.

willing or unable to make the journey to the parish church at Clerkenwell Green. In 1854 Pentonville was made a separate parish. Peculiar to the church was an annual service for circus clowns: this stemmed from the fact that Joseph Grimaldi was buried in the churchyard. The building is now demolished.

Claremont Chapel was built for the Congregationalists in 1819 using funds provided by Thomas Wilson of Highbury.

Apart from Grimaldi, Pentonville was home to at least two other famous people. John Stuart Mill, the philosopher, was born at what became 39 Rodney Street, in 1806; the house was demolished in 1957. Thomas Carlyle, one of the most celebrated writers of his day, spent at least ten years in the area before moving to Chelsea in 1834, where he stayed for the rest of his life. He lived in Claremont Square, Myddelton Square and then Calshot Street. Thereafter he gradually moved westwards into the King's Cross and upper Bloomsbury areas.

53. *The east entrance to the Islington tunnel.* From a watercolour by Thomas Hosmer Shepherd.

The Regent's Canal

The Regent's Canal came rather late to the canal scene. Its function was to link the Grand Junction Canal, which ran from the Midlands to the west of London, and the new West India Docks on the Thames. The first, westerly, stretch was opened in 1816 and the Islington section, the City Road Basin and the connection to the Thames were finished in 1820. The opening ceremony included an aquatic procession. Barges and boats were decorated with streamers, and salutes were sounded as they emerged from the blackness of the Islington tunnel.

The toast drunk at the ceremony was 'Prosperity to the Regent's Canal' but the Company had only a few years to recoup its investment before the railways inexorably bit into its trade and profits. Furthermore, its construction had been dogged by inaccurate estimates, a poor supply of water, a lack of capital, embezzlement by the superintendent of the works, and an acrimonious law suit by a landholder in St Pancras. Not the least of the engineering problems was the construction of a tunnel for much of the Islington stretch. This begins just east of Caledonian Road, goes beneath the lower part of Barnsbury, and daylight is next encountered between Noel Road and Vincent Terrace. At one point it passes under the New River in a strata particularly rich in fossils – the remains of a crocodile were found during the canal's excavations at Islington. This stretch, before the advent of automatic power, was covered by a company crew who propelled the boat with their legs while laying on planks laid outwards from each bow, pushing against the sides of the tunnel. In 1826 a steam-driven barge was brought into service which could take through the tunnel a number of other barges roped together. A lurid description exists of the experience in the pitch black tunnel, of the noise of the steam barge, the sound of the barges smacking against the sides of the tunnel, and the smoke generated by the engine.

The City Road Basin was built to encourage traffic. Old maps show numerous timber wharves here, the canal being an ideal carrier for wood off-loaded at Limehouse and transported for finishing to the City Road. Many of the warehouses of this time still survive and the whole area, much neglected for years, is now being regenerated.

54. *The Regent's Canal from Maiden Lane.* A view published in 1819. Maiden Lane is now called York Way.

The Building of Highbury

56. *Highbury Place*. An engraving published in 1835.

Around the beginning of the 14th century the moated manor house for Highbury was located approximately on the site of today's Leigh Road. It was granted to the Knights Hospitallers of Clerkenwell and was used by the prior as a country house, but the general unpopularity of such religious establishments, particularly that of the Hospitallers, resulted in the house becoming a suburban casualty of the Peasants' Revolt of 1381. The mob burnt the priory at Clerkenwell and later proceeded to Highbury where the house met the same fate. For the next few centuries the derelict site was known as Jack Straw's Castle, named from one of the leaders of the Revolt.

Development in Highbury began in the 1770s when a stockbroker called John Dawes took out building leases. At the same time he filled in part of the old moat and built himself Highbury House on the site of the old manor house; this was bought by Alexander Aubert in 1788. Here he indulged his in-

Above:
57. *Highbury Terrace*. An engraving published in 1835.

Bottom left:
58. *Highbury Grange*. Late 19th-century photograph.

Facing page, top:
59. *Highbury College*. Originally a college for nonconformist clergy, it was later purchased by the Church of England for training purposes.

Facing page, bottom:
60. *Highbury Place*. From a postcard *c*1905.

terest in astronomy, and here he built himself a well-equipped observatory which was much envied. The house lasted until 1939, when Eton Court was built on its site.

Highbury Place, fronting what became Highbury Fields, was the first development. Designed by John Spiller, it was built by 1777. Famous residents have included the politician Joseph Chamberlain from 1845–c1854 at No.25, and at No.1 Walter Sickert ran a studio and art school from 1927–31. Highbury Terrace followed in 1789; it was then rather isolated.

Dissenting religion thrived in Highbury. Early in

Highbury Place, N.

61. *Highbury Crescent*. An early 19th-century engraving.

the 18th century the Highbury Society, a group of non-conformists, met here, and it is not surprising that the area was chosen in 1825 to build Highbury College, a training school for clergy. The irony is that it lasted but a short time and was sold to the Church of England to be used to teach *their* clergy. This building, shown in *Illustration 59*, was designed by John Davies, very much in the style of the British Museum. It was gutted by fire in 1946, and replaced by flats. Its grounds had already been purchased by Arsenal, a football club, which was originally associated with the Woolwich Arsenal south of the river, and which came to Highbury in 1913.

Highbury Fields were, in the 18th century, freehold property but in the ups and downs of property speculation escaped development; they were purchased for the public in 1885.

62. *Joseph Chamberlain*. From an ink drawing by Phil May.

63. *The Islington Turnpike entrance to London.*

The Turnpike Roads

The Islington Turnpike stood at various points between White Lion Street and Liverpool Road until it was abolished in 1864. It was regarded as being more decorative than most. The Islington Turnpike Trust, (also known as the Highgate and Hampstead Trust), was set up in 1716 and by 1735 controlled, in Islington, the High Street and Upper Street, Essex, Holloway, Liverpool and Ball's Pond Roads, and Highgate Hill. In the early 19th century more turnpike roads were added – the New North Road, Archway Road, Caledonian Road, and Camden/Seven Sisters Road.

In a spot census of vehicles using the Islington gate in 1856 there were counted 2792 in 24 hours. Turnpikes were simple enough to control when roads were sparse, but as development occurred around London it was possible to circumvent the gates by the use of new side roads. This led to the erection of irritating bars at one end of the new side roads to prevent this. Other turnpikes were in Holloway Road by the junction with Liverpool Road, and in Ball's Pond Road at the junction with Essex Road.

After a long campaign almost all the principal turnpike gates were abolished on one day in July 1864 and the roads made the responsibility of the parishes. One of the last toll roads in London to be freed, in 1876, was the Archway Road.

64. *Islington Turnpike*. A watercolour by Maund.

65. *Islington Turnpike*. A view published in 1819.

More New Developments

Above:
66. *Near the Caledonian Asylum, Caledonian Road.* A watercolour by 'E.H.D.' painted in 1838. It is difficult to identify the location of the artist. The position of the Asylum, north of today's Pentonville Prison on the same side of the road, is known. Also, as there is high ground in the distance, presumably the view is towards the north. However, Caledonian Road has always been straight and the curve depicted in the road is puzzling.

Below:
67. *The Caledonian Asylum.* An engraving published in 1835.

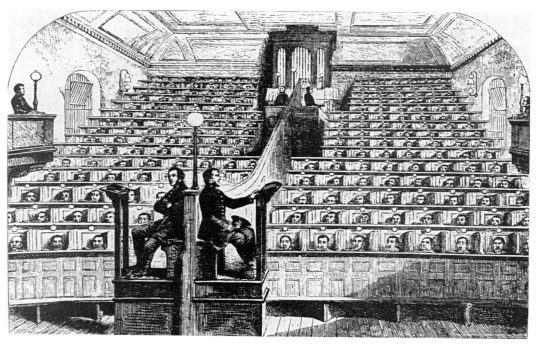

68. *The chapel at Pentonville Prison*. The prisoners are sat in pews with high sides so that they are unable to see their neighbours once their masks are removed. The guards are on prominent display.

Facing page:
69. *A Map of Islington parish*. Originally published in 1805 and revised *c*1830.

Caledonian Road was a speculative venture laid out by the Battle Bridge and Holloway Road Company to provide a link between Euston Road and Holloway Road. Its name then was the Chalk Road. It was built in 1826, mainly through fields – *Illustration 66* depicts just how rural it was at the time. It was not until the 1840s that a number of terraces were built. Before that, however, an orphanage called the Royal Caledonian Asylum, 'for the sons of indigent Scots killed on active service', was established on a site just north of today's Pentonville Prison and on which local authority housing now stands. From this the road eventually took its name. The orphanage had been opened in 1819 in Hatton Garden but soon outgrew its premises. When the building shown in *Illustration 67*, designed by George Tappen, was opened, both boys and girls were resident here. In 1903 the Asylum moved to Bushey, the building was demolished and a particularly ugly LCC estate put on its site and grounds.

Pentonville Prison was built in 1842, the same year as parts of nearby Barnsbury, and it is likely that the nearness of the prison deterred the building of good class houses north of Arundel Square. Surprisingly, bearing in mind the regime and the suffering of the prisoners, Pentonville was the culmination of efforts by prison reformers, notably Howard and Bentham, whose ideas as to the reformation of criminals gained influence. The belief grew that many criminals could be cured by solitude and silence. When prisoners first entered Pentonville they endured 18 months on their own; any contact with other prisoners, even by tapping on the walls, risked punishment. A smile, a gesture or a whisper would bring a term in the dark basement of the prison. The prohibition on contact was taken to extremes – prisoners in the chapel were prevented by the construction of the pews from seeing other inmates. It is not surprising that numerous cases of madness are recorded in Pentonville and other prisons which followed its example. Each prisoner was allowed one visit for a quarter of an hour every six months, and one letter during the same period. Even this way of life was a watered-down version of Bentham's earlier plan, where inmates worked sixteen hours daily and were under observation all the time.

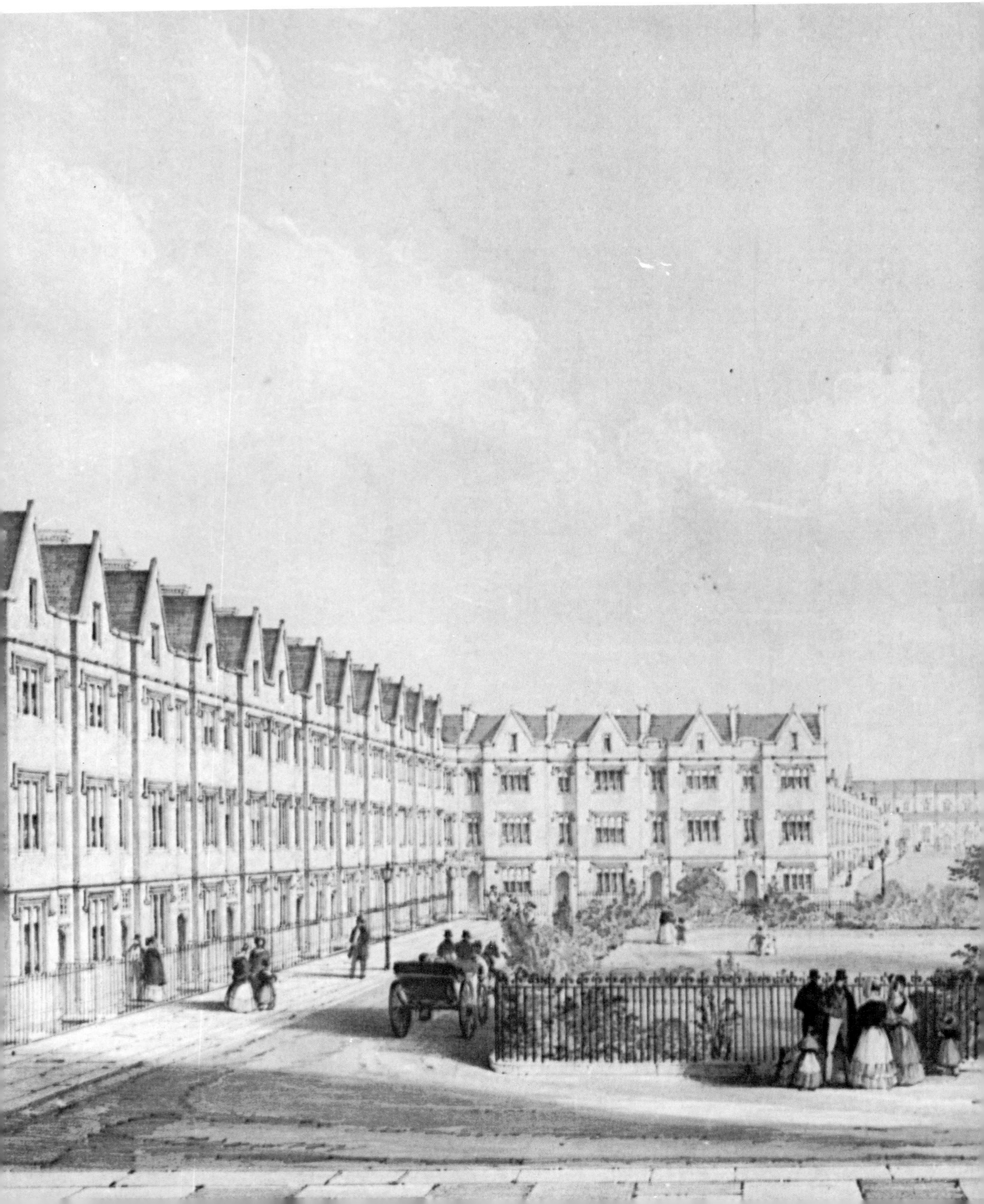

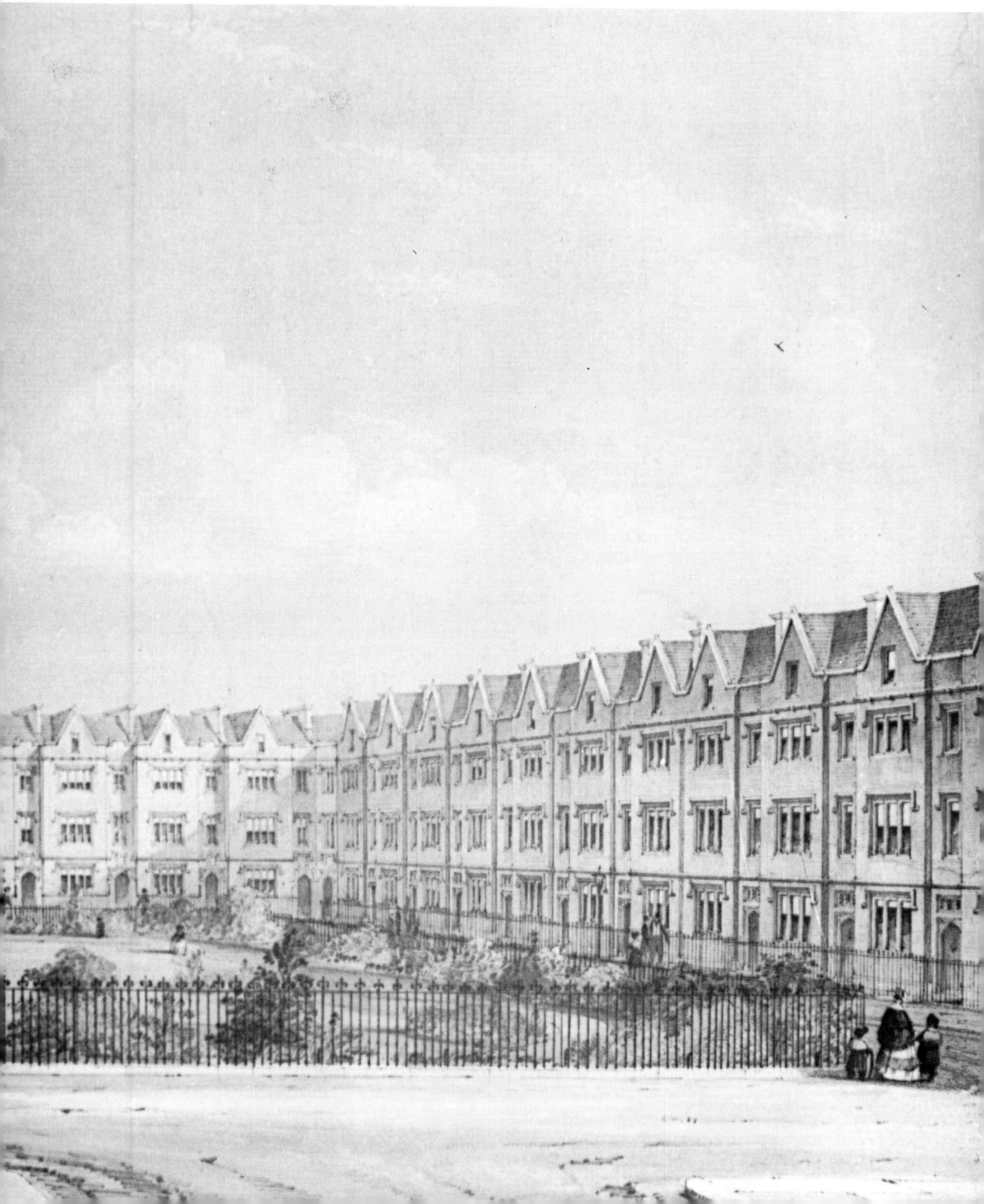

"Hornsey Row," Islington.
On the East side of the Upper Street, between Tyndale Place and Canonbury Lane.
The two end houses, also the shops, are modern: The greater part was
pulled down in Dec.r 1884.

J.D.W. Oct.r 1884.

Hornsey Row
1769

Previous pages:
70. *Lonsdale Square.* A view soon after the Square was built in *c*1841.

71. *Hornsey Row, Islington.* This row, owned by a charity administered by Hornsey parish, was apparently built in 1769. The caption on this illustration reads: 'On the east side of the Upper Street, between Tyndale Place and Canonbury Lane. The two end houses, also the shops, are modern. The greater part was pulled down in Decr. 1884.'

Facing page:
72. *A Plan of St James's District, Islington, 1839.* This was evidently a plan of the area covered by the new parish of St James, Chillingworth Street. It stretches from today's Offord Road to Mackenzie Road and Holloway Road. The Pentonville Prison, opened in 1842, is being built, the Chalk Road, (today's Caledonian Road), is to the west of that and Pocock's Fields cover today's Arundel Square, Ellington and Bride Streets.

The parish map of *c*1830, *(Illustration 69)*, shows little development since the previous plan of 1735. The beginnings of Barnsbury are seen in Cloudesley Square; Liverpool Road has sprouted terraces, as too has the farther end of Upper Street. One of these terraces in Upper Street, south of Canonbury Lane, is pictured in *Illustration 71*. The land here was owned by a charity vested in Hornsey parish in 1659, and the income from the rents of these buildings went towards the apprenticing of six poor boys in the City of London.

The Albion Tea House, in today's Thornhill Road, may be seen with what was called Gosseyfield to its rear; this was used for cattle and was the site of today's Lonsdale Square. This unusual square was designed by Richard Cromwell Carpenter and was first occupied in 1842.

The second Islington workhouse may be seen in Barnsbury Street and across Liverpool Road was a building called the Church Missionary College, built in 1825 on the site of a botanic garden; Sutton Dwellings now occupy its site.

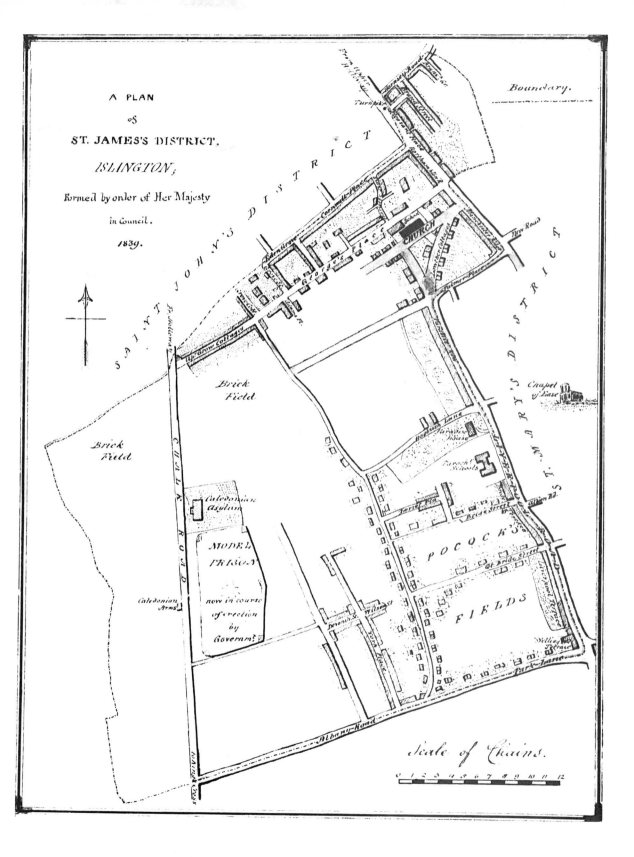

A PLAN

of

ST. JAMES'S DISTRICT,

ISLINGTON;

Formed by order of Her Majesty

in Council.

1839.

Scale of Chains.

73. *A 19th-century photograph of Laycock's Dairy off Liverpool Road*. Liverpool Buildings are in the background.

74. *Laycock's Dairy, Liverpool Road*. A 19th-century advertisement.

The plan of St. James's District, *(Illustration 72)*, was compiled in 1839 when a new parish district was formed for St. James's church in Chillingworth Street. The chapel-of-ease to the right is the church of St. Mary Magdalene still, then, part of the main parish, and to the left is the Caledonian Asylum and Pentonville prison in the process of being built. Albany Road/Park Lane at the bottom is the route of today's Offord Road and above this we have Pocock's Fields. The Pocock family were large developers in north London. They built an early part of Kilburn, for example, and almost certainly built the streets from Ellington Street to Offord Road, which fell victim in social status to the nearness of the prison and the advent of the North London Railway.

75. *Amwell Street.* From a postcard c1905. The view looks north towards Claremont Square.

Across Liverpool Road is Mr Laycock's dairy farm which, his business card shown in *Illustration 74* proclaims, was founded in 1720; it was a notable feature in the area and particularly used by drovers when they needed to leave their cattle overnight before Smithfield.

South of the Pentonville Road, in what was then the parish of Clerkenwell, the Lloyd Baker estate was being built. This land, too, had once been part of the property of the Knights Hospitallers and had found its way into the possession of the Bishop of St. Asaph, Dr. William Lloyd, in the reign of James II. His great granddaughter married a Rev. William Baker in 1775, and he and his son began developing their land from 1819. Much of it survives intact, probably due to the family possession of the estate into the 1970s, when modern conservation laws protected it. Some steps running from Granville Square to King's Cross, now bridged by Ryan's Hotel, were immortalised by Arnold Bennett in his *Riceyman's Steps*.

The Lloyd Baker Estate is flanked on one side by Amwell Street, which is partly on New River Company land. Once again, because the land on either side of the road has been held by two non-acquisitive owners, development has been ignored until the time when a local outcry could probably prevent it. Clerkenwell Parochial School, founded in 1700, has been in its Amwell Street building, designed by William C. Milne, since 1830.

76. *Thornhill Crescent.* A photograph taken *c*1930.

The Thornhill Estate derives its name from a family with land also in Huntingdonshire and Cambridgeshire, a fact which has given Barnsbury some of those counties' place names. George Thornhill, M.P., built part of Richmond Avenue and then Hemingford Road by the 1840s. Thornhill Square, begun in 1848, is really a rounded and irregular rectangle of generous proportions, surmounted by Thornhill Crescent. It was built in the very late 1840s and the church of St. Andrew, designed by Francis Newman and John Johnson, was consecrated in 1854. The Square remains substantially as planned, other than the 1907 insertion of a branch library. Thornhill Road on the other hand, (it confusingly includes Barnsbury Square and not Thornhill Square as one would expect), was built bit by bit to no particular scheme in groups of villas as speculators felt able.

Barnsbury Square contains the most imposing Mountford House, alleged, mistakenly, to be on the site of a Roman camp but almost certainly on that of a moated manor house. The house has been spoilt by the addition of a factory building to the rear and one doubts if it will ever regain its splendour. To either side of it are Mountford Crescent and Terrace, both set around private gardens in a way most unusual for Islington.

77. *St. Paul's Road, Canonbury.* From a postcard *c*1905.

St. Paul's Road, originally called Hopping Lane, was a carriageway only, without footway on either side. This may well explain the narrowness of the present pavements and the uncomfortable closeness of the terraces to the roadway. St. Paul's church, located on the corner with Essex Road, was designed by Sir Charles Barry and opened in 1828. The road continues into Ball's Pond Road, the subject of many music-hall jokes, named from a nearby pond owned by John Ball in the 17th century; Ball kept a tavern here as well. When this road went through open fields it was favoured as a location for several alms-houses.

78. *The Union Chapel, Compton Terrace.* From an engraving published in 1835. The first four houses of Compton Terrace are shown.

Compton Terrace began in 1806 as two houses on both sides of the Union Chapel; it was built by Henry Leroux of Stoke Newington, who later went bankrupt and then recovered to build Canonbury Square. The Terrace was eventually built five houses longer than are there today: in 1944 a V2 rocket fell at the Highbury Corner end, causing severe damage in the area and the eventual demolition of the five end houses. One wonders how the Highbury roundabout would have been built had it not been for this incident!

The Chapel, designed to take 1000 at a sitting, was opulently furnished, and was the property of a Congregational assembly which had formed in Highbury in 1799. The Chapel also established a school for 100 pupils and a 'Maternal Society' to supply poor women with child-bed linen.

The Chapel's replacement of 1877, an even larger building, was designed by James Cubitt, with the extraordinary tower being added in 1889. Incorporated into the interior is a portion of the Plymouth Rock, upon which the Pilgrim Fathers landed in America in 1620, and which was presented to the Chapel by the Pilgrim Society of America in 1883.

The maps of Islington for the 19th century show all sorts of churches that have long disappeared or else now serve other purposes. One such was the North London Synagogue, opened in what is now Lofting Road in 1868. It was eventually demolished in 1960, when Barnes Court was built on its site. Union Chapel, described on page 66, was not the only Congregational chapel around. One existed in Offord Road and still stands, very run-down and used as a decorating warehouse. Another stood on the corner of Barnsbury Street and Milner Square, and yet another was built in Westbourne Road at the corner of Bride Street. A sect called the Sandemanians had a chapel where the telephone exchange stands off Roman Way, and another in Furlong Road in which the Conservative Party recently had a headquarters.

79. *The North London Synagogue, Lofting Road.* From the *Illustrated London News*, 3rd October, 1868.

The Stonefields estate, consisting of 16 acres to the west of Liverpool Road, was bequeathed to the parish by Richard Cloudesley in 1518. The income from that bequest is still used today for charitable purposes. Cloudesley evidently did not die with peace of mind. The belief then that masses for one's soul could procure its reception into heaven, led to a great many charitable bequests linked to a condition that masses would be chanted at certain times on behalf of the soul of the deceased. Cloudesley, however, seemed to be saying in his will that only quantity would overcome resistance at the portals, for he asked for a thousand masses to be said 'incontinently after my decease, as hastily as may be', in his anxiety to join the select hosts. This did not appear to quiet his spirit, however, for it was believed that its restlessness was responsible for some minor earthquakes in the 16th century in the vicinity of the parish churchyard where he was buried, and exorcists at dead of night decided to resolve the matter.

The Estate was the first in Barnsbury to be built upon and like much of inner London, was turned into a brickfield first.

80. *Brickmaking on the Stonefields estate.* Liverpool Road is to the right and the parish workhouse in Barnsbury Street is in the distance.

81. *Fisher's House, Essex Road.* View from the garden. This house was demolished in 1845.

Fisher House stood on the site of Nos. 100–102 Essex Road until *c*1845. This substantial building was purchased by Sir Richard Fisher in 1680, and by inheritance and purchase was eventually owned by a Halton and a Pickering, both of whom are commemorated in local street names. From 1807–36 the house was used for a private lunatic asylum.

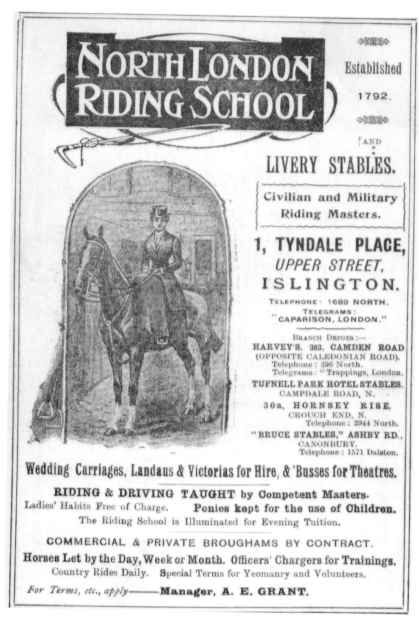

82. *Advertisement for the North London Riding School, 1 Tyndale Place, Upper Street.*

83. *Offord Road, Barnsbury*. From a postcard of *c*1905.

Many street names in Barnsbury and Canonbury reflect the ownership of the fields by a number of families. There are various *Offords* in the county of *Huntingdon* where the *Thornhill* family had its seat. *Matilda*, the wife of George Thornhill, came from *Hemingford* Grey in the same county. On the other side of Liverpool Road, Thomas *Milner Gibson* of *Theberton* Hall, Suffolk held the land. In Canonbury the Northampton family included the names *Spencer*, *Compton*, and *Alwyne*. Other names, such as Almeida and Waterloo obviously commemorate battles, but Lofting Road (previously John Street) marks an obscure London merchant who began the first thimble factory in Islington in 1695. That part of Lofting Road renamed Bridgeman Road in recent years remembers the Rev. Arthur Bridgeman, vicar of St. Andrew, Thornhill Square, 1872–93. Ripplevale Grove pays tribute to Sir John French, Earl of Ypres, who was born in Ripple Vale, Kent and William Belitha was a small landholder off Barnsbury Road. Anne *Packington*, widow, left land off the Essex Road to the Clothworkers' Company in 1559. Sir Henry *Mildmay*, a civil servant in the reign of Charles I, married the daughter of an Islington landholder.

84. *Hemingford Road, Barnsbury.* From a postcard of *c*1905.

85. *From a map of Islington, c.1853.*

Islington at Prayer

Until the 18th century Islington had only one place of worship, that of the parish church of St. Mary in Upper Street. A certain amount of nonconformity flourished in Islington, as it did in other north London suburbs, but not sufficiently to warrant a chapel. Some forty nonconformist Protestants had been arrested in 1558 at a private service in a field in Islington, of whom 13 were subsequently burnt, but we do not know if these were local people or had merely come to Islington to escape detection. John Wesley and George Whitefield were invited by the vicar to preach at St. Mary's in 1738, only to scandalize the churchwardens who tried to prohibit a recurrence. Henceforth these two famous preachers occasionally used private houses in Islington in which to air their views. A number of ministers, ejected from their livings in the reign of Charles II, moved to Islington where they founded Dissenting academies, but the first Dissenting chapel was not built until 1744, in the Essex Road. This was followed by Islington Chapel in what is now Gaskin Street in 1788, and, as we have seen on *page 66*, the Congregationalist Union Chapel in Compton Terrace was built in 1806.

All sorts of sects flourished in Islington – twenty of them were registered in 1870, with names such as Liberal Catholics, Paracletians, Sandemanians or Glasites, and Seventh-day Baptists. The Baptists, the Salvation Army and the various sections of the Methodists all competed with these for the hearts of the many poor and destitute in the parish as the population increased dramatically throughout the century.

Roman Catholicism returned to Islington in 1837 when two priests from a church in Moorfields opened a school in Duncan Street, which was also used for worship. From this developed the magnificent church of St John the Evangelist, designed by J.J. Scoles, which opened in 1843. The increase in the Irish population, particularly in the poorer and northern parts of Islington, resulted in the Catholic enclave around Eden Grove and the purchase of an inn on Highgate Hill on whose site St Joseph's was later built.

As for the established church, it was dividing and sub-dividing its parish. From the one parish of St. Mary at the beginning of the 18th century stemmed numerous others, the process reversing itself in the 20th century as churchgoing contracted and two or more parishes combined together. In common with other such areas in London, Islington is generally richer for the buildings if, at times, it is not known quite what to do with those which have become redundant. Some have been converted to commercial use, at least one has become a theatre, at least two have become apartments, and others have simply been neglected so long that they have had to be demolished. Not all the buildings, of course, were distinguished, but it would be a pity to lose the Holloway Baptist Church, now visibly becoming derelict on the Holloway Road, and it was a shame to lose the church of St Michael by Roumieu in Bingfield Street, off Caledonian Road.

86. *Building the first Islington Chapel in Gaskin Street.*

The first Islington Chapel, for the use of nonconforming Protestants, was built in Gaskin Street in 1788 at the expense of John Ives, a local blacksmith. A new building replaced it in 1815 at the corner with Upper Street; this was allowed its own burial ground two years later. When Upper Street was widened in 1889 the present Chapel was erected to the designs of Bonella and Paul. This was closed in 1979.

87. *Holy Trinity, Cloudesley Square.* From a postcard *c*1905.

Holy Trinity, designed by Sir Charles Barry, was the first Barnsbury church. Considering just how small was the population of Cloudesley Square and the streets built on the Cloudesley Estate, it was a generous provision. Its style is taken from that of King's College, Cambridge. Since 1980 it has been used by the Pentecostal Celestial Church of Christ.

Around the corner are the offices of Dove Brothers, the builders. This old-established Islington business was founded by William Spencer Dove, a jobbing carpenter, when he arrived in London in 1824. His first major contracts in Islington were the Islington Literary and Scientific Institution in Almeida Street, (now the Almeida Theatre), and much of Milner Square. By the 1870s the company possessed 12 horses, premises in Moon and Studd Streets, and two steam engines. Dove Brothers built about 130 London churches, including at least 15 in Islington.

88. *The Chapel-of-Ease, later St Mary Magdalene, Holloway Road.* From an engraving published in 1835.

As the number of residents increased and parish churches were found wanting in accommodation it was common to construct a 'chapel-of-ease' in another part of the parish where there was a considerable population. By making this chapel a subsidiary of the mother church, instead of a parish church in its own right, the vicar of the parish was able to retain the proceeds of the collection-box and the fees for christenings, marriages and burials. In Islington, such a chapel was built on the Holloway Road in 1814, to the designs of William Wickings; in

time this became St. Mary Magdalene with a parish of its own, but its original function was to serve the people of Holloway. Even so there must have been enough residents in Upper Holloway still deserting to churches outside after that because yet another church was built in the Holloway Road in 1828. This was St. John's, designed by Charles Barry. A glance at the map of the parish of about 1830 suggests that this was an odd siting for such a large church because it is surrounded by fields and is in direct competition for a congregation with the equally large chapel-of-

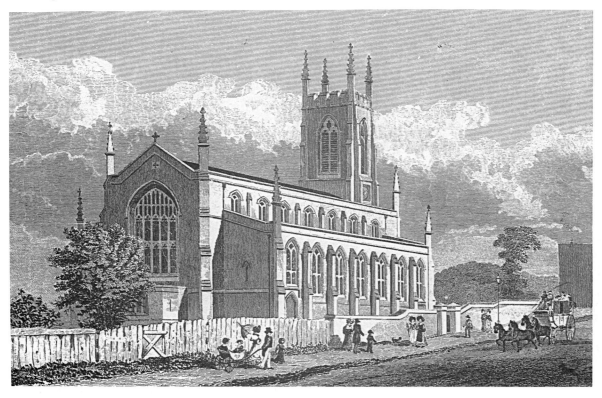

89. *St. John's church, Holloway Road.* From an engraving by Thomas Hosmer Shepherd.

Facing page:
90. *St Andrew's church, Thornhill Square.* From a postcard *c*1905.

Facing page:
91. *St David's church, Westbourne Road.* From a postcard *c*1905. To the right is the school which still exists. A placard on the front is advertising the fact that an evening school is now open. In the distance is Mackenzie Road.

ease. Barry, later to be the architect for the new Houses of Parliament, had a busy year in 1828. Apart from St. John's, his other churches of St. Paul's, Essex Road and Holy Trinity, Cloudesley Square, were also consecrated. The other principal architect of Islington churches was A.D. Gough, who built St. Jude, Mildmay Park, St. Mark, Tollington Park and St. Matthew, Essex Road; also, together with Roumieu, he built Milner Square. Almost invariably his builder was Dove Brothers of Islington. Smaller churches to serve particular areas came in the next wave of church building in the 1850s and 1860s. St. George, Tufnell Park, designed by George Truefitt, has survived and has been used, since it closed, for theatre-in-the-round. St. Clement's and St. David's, both in Westbourne Road, are good examples of neighbourhood churches, the former quite distinguished as it was built by George Gilbert Scott. Happily it has been saved from the twin enemies of weather and vandalism and has been converted into apartments in a rather more sympathetic way than is the case with one of the earlier local churches, that of St. James, Chillingworth Street.

St. Andrew's Church Thornhill Square Barnsbury

St. Davids Church Westbourne Rd. Barnsbury

Caring for the Poor

Until 1824 Islington was governed by an Open Vestry, that is, any male ratepayer could attend meetings of the Vestry and vote. This was not popular with the wealthier inhabitants and an Act was procured in 1824 under which a Select Vestry was appointed by only the highest rated residents. This undemocratic way continued until 1855 when the Vestry was obliged to adopt a system whereby the parish was divided into wards, each returning vestrymen, and in which the franchise was considerably extended. This reorganisation and the acceptance of a proper role for the Vestry led to the belated erection of a Vestry Hall in 1859, on the present site of the petrol station in Upper Street at the junction with Florence Street. In 1927 this Hall was sold and became a Lido Cinema, later an Odeon; it was demolished in 1961. The first part of the present Town Hall, architect E.C.P. Monson, was opened in 1923.

92. *The Islington Vestry Hall, Upper Street.* A petrol station now occupies the site.

93. *Islington Workhouse, Barnsbury Street.* From an engraving published in 1819.

The Vestry rented a house for their poor in 1726, in Stroud Green, and a few years later opened a second house in Holloway Road near the junction with Liverpool Road. As in other inner London areas, the problem of the poor was overwhelming the primitive vestry system and the resources of the community. A new and enlarged building was built in 1777 in Barnsbury Street near the junction with Liverpool Road, on land donated to the parish. This remained throughout the development of Barnsbury, seemingly without causing a blight on the quality of the new terraces, and subsequently moved in the 1860s to a much larger building in St. John's Road, Upper Holloway. The Workhouse in Barnsbury Street is shown in *Illustration 93*. Enshrined in the rules was the belief, which still has much currency today, that the poor may be categorised and divided into those who are destitute from misfortune and those who are in the workhouse because of their own laziness and vice. The administrators of the Workhouse were urged "That in the placing of persons into their several wards, as well as in other respects, some distinction be made between such poor as have been creditable housekeepers, and reduced by misfortunes, and the other poor who became so by vice or idleness". The removal of the workhouse enabled the Vestry to build a yard and, on the corner, a Poor Relief office allied with a Dispensary for the poor. The latter building, of eccentric architecture, is still there and was recently sold at auction.

Instituted 1807.

LONDON FEMALE PENITENTIARY, PENTONVILLE.

LONDON FEMALE PENITENTIARY, SUPPORTED BY VOLUNTARY CONTRIBUTIONS.

The Laundry.   The present House.   The wing now erecting.

The intended side Building
for the Prompt Reception Ward & Infirmary.

Part of the intended Quadrangle which with the front Building
will gradually inclose the Ground.

Scale of Feet

SUPPORTED by VOLUNTARY CONTRIBUTIONS.

94. *An appeal brochure for the London Female Penitentiary, Pentonville Road.*

95. *Peabody Square, off Essex Road.* From the *Illustrated London News*, 10th March, 1866.

The hardship of early 19th-century life led many women to prostitution. One popular remedy of those concerned with this was to have a building in which such women might live where they could first be penitent, and then be taught useful work whereby they could make a living when they left. There were a number of such establishments in London, supported by charity and a strong moral tone. Charles Dickens, for example, helped to organise one for the Baroness Burdett-Coutts in which the Baroness joylessly forbad the women to wear anything but the plainest and dreariest of clothes. Another large penitentiary existed in Highgate Village, which survived until 1940.

The establishment shown in an appeal advertisement here, *(Illustration 94)*, was founded in Blackfriars in 1807. The same year it acquired No.166 Pentonville Road, a large house built for a John Cumming Esq, and which had latterly been used as a school for Catholic girls. The inmates of the Penitentiary had to exhibit a genuine desire to reform and in the regime of work and religion to show no 'refractory disposition or unmanageable temper'. In a report of 1863 it was computed that 4172 women had stayed at the Penitentiary since 1807. Of these about 1400 had been placed in domestic service, over 900 had been reconciled to friends or families, over 600 had left at their own request, and 31 had died. In 1884 the establishment moved to Stoke Newington.

The origin of the numerous Peabody Buildings in London is a gift from the American philanthropist, George Peabody, to help the London poor. Unfortunately the Trust chose as its first and principal architect Henry Darbishire, whose austere ideas as to architecture for the poor left a depressing heritage. (On the other hand, Darbishire could design entertainly, as the eccentric Holly Village in Highgate shows.) When supervising similar buildings for Baroness Burdett-Coutts in the East End, it is alleged he purposely allowed gaps between doors and jambs to ensure that the lower classes took in fresh air.

The first Peabody Buildings opened in Commercial Street, E1 in 1864. The blocks off Essex Road and Greenman Street, shown in *Illustration 95*, were opened two years later. There are 155 dwellings in the four blocks, intended for over 650 people.

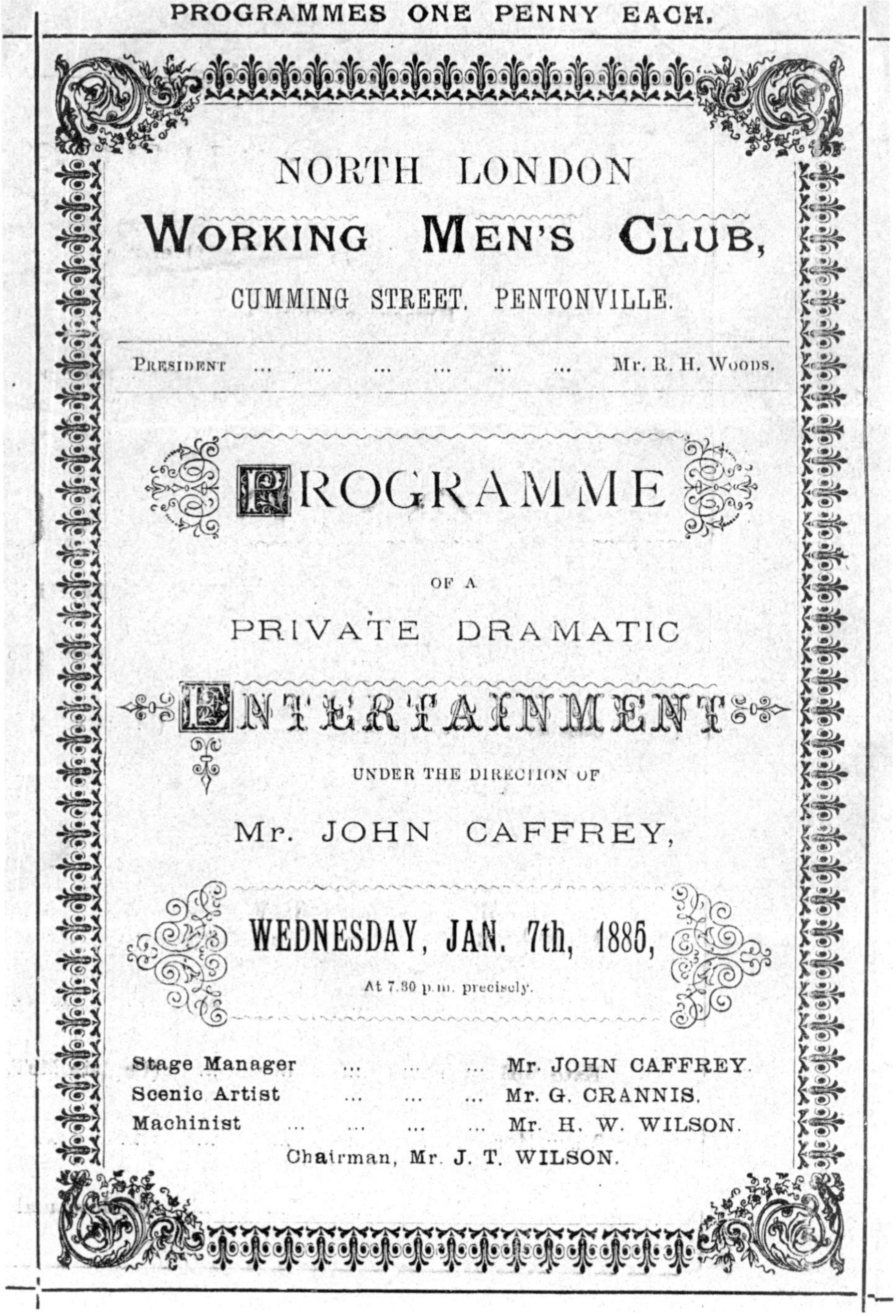

PROGRAMMES ONE PENNY EACH.

NORTH LONDON
WORKING MEN'S CLUB,
CUMMING STREET, PENTONVILLE.

PRESIDENT ... ... Mr. R. H. WOODS.

PROGRAMME

OF A

PRIVATE DRAMATIC

ENTERTAINMENT

UNDER THE DIRECTION OF

Mr. JOHN CAFFREY,

WEDNESDAY, JAN. 7th, 1885,

At 7.30 p.m. precisely.

Stage Manager ... ... Mr. JOHN CAFFREY.
Scenic Artist ... ... Mr. G. CRANNIS.
Machinist ... ... Mr. H. W. WILSON.

Chairman, Mr. J. T. WILSON.

96. *Programme for a Private Dramatic Entertainment at the Working Men's Club, Cumming Street, Pentonville, 7th January, 1885.*
The dramatic evening consisted of an overture, a humorous song and a comedy in three acts called *'Old Soldiers'*.

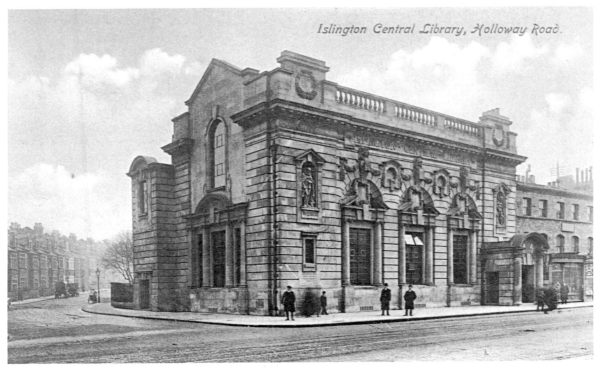

Islington Central Library, Holloway Road.

97. *Islington Central Library, Holloway Road.* From a postcard *c*1930.

Free public libraries came slowly to London: the example set by large provincial cities, and the less than enthusiastic encouragement of the government, enabled the London vestries to delay the matter as long as possible. The method of doing this was to hold a local referendum on the adoption of the Public Libraries Act 1855 and, as the voters were usually those who paid most of the rates and were affluent enough to buy their own books, free libraries, as far as they were concerned, could be left to charity. At public meetings in Islington in 1870 and 1874 the adoption of the Act was voted down at public meetings, in the latter year by a majority of 1000. It was not until the advent of Andrew Carnegie that the ratepayers of Islington adopted the Act.

Islington's recalcitrance was not unusual in London, indeed it was the norm, and the millionaire Carnegie sought to overcome this by offering money to borough councils to fund a library on condition that they found a site and paid for the ongoing costs. This enticed quite a few councils, resigned anyway to the inevitable. Islington opened their first branch in Manor Gardens, in a building designed by Henry Hare, in 1906. Even so, a large part of the book stock was donated by the Unitarian Free Library on High-gate Hill and Islington, what with this and the Carnegie money, got their first free library very cheaply. Henry Hare also designed the Central Library in Holloway Road, which opened the following year. This grandiose structure, shown in *Illustration 97*, now has its entrance in Fieldway Crescent where a quite inappropriate modern addition has been built. Also in 1907, the Council, swiftly making amends for their tardiness, opened yet another branch in what was then Lofting Road. This was designed by A. Beresford Pite.

When the Great Northern Hospital moved from the Caledonian Road up to Holloway Road, its old site was taken by Islington Vestry on which to erect its first public baths in 1892. It contained three swimming baths, one of which doubled up as a hall during the winter, and there were also facilities for laundry work. Essex Road Baths, shown above, were opened in 1895 and the building has only recently been demolished.

Hornsey Road Baths opened in 1892 as well. This received bomb damage in the last war and has since been modernised. There has been an open-air swimming bath at Highbury Fields since 1921. This was replaced by the present, much admired, building in 1984.

98. *The interior of the old Essex Road Washhouses.*

The London Fever Hospital was founded at King's Cross in 1802. Against local opposition, which had good reason to be wary of an infectious diseases hospital in its midst, it moved to Liverpool Road in 1848 into a building designed by Charles Fowler, the architect of the Covent Garden market building. This hospital was intended for the treatment of poor people suffering from contagious fever. Eventually it became part of the Royal Free which, on its centralisation at Hampstead, left a trail of redundant buildings behind. Fowler's building is now shamefully neglected and abandoned, and its future still uncertain.

99. *The London Fever Hospital, Liverpool Road.*

100. *The Royal Northern Hospital, Holloway Road.* From *The Builder*, 25th December, 1886.

The Royal Northern Hospital in Holloway Road began as the Great Northern Hospital in York Way opposite the entrance to the Great Northern terminus of King's Cross, very near, indeed, to the first site of the London Fever Hospital. It was established by a young surgeon called Sherard Statham in 1856, at his own expense, for the treatment of poor people in north London. After a year the number of beds was increased to 50 and the lack of money was overcome by voluntary work on the part of the medical staff. In 1862 the site was bought by the Metropolitan Railway and with the proceeds the hospital moved to other premises and eventually to the site of the swimming baths in Caledonian Road. One of the doctors here was the future Poet Laureate, Robert Bridges. The contact between the hospital and the Great Northern and the Metropolitan railways was cultivated, to the extent that those companies sent their staff for treatment there; this, in turn, encouraged donations from the companies to expand the hospital. In 1888 it moved to its present site in the Holloway Road, to a new building designed by Keith Young and Henry Hall.

The first fire brigades were those which belonged to fire insurance companies. Their customers displayed plaques, or fire-marks, on the exterior of their houses to ensure that the appropriate brigade, when summoned, would feel obliged to fight the fire. From 1833 some of the larger companies combined forces in the London Fire Engine Establishment, whose main pre-occupation was the saving of property rather than lives. At the same time there were many voluntary fire brigades, such as the one shown in *Illustration 101*, mostly deriving from the initiative of the vestries, but quite often formed as a result of local agitation when the vestry failed to supply facilities.

Islington Vestry kept its own engine in the church-yard, and then on Islington Green, with one in Holloway at an unspecified spot, but no doubt near the junction with Liverpool Road. The Metropolitan (later London) Fire Brigade was formed in 1866 and Islington supplied a temporary station in Florence Street; the present fire station in Upper Street was built in 1900.

101. *Holloway Volunteer Fire Brigade.*

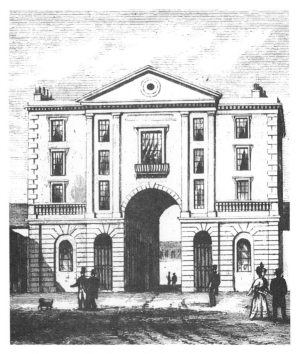

102. *Entrance to the Islington Cattle Market, off Essex Road.*

The Cattle Markets

103. *The Metropolitan Cattle Market, Market Road.*

The problems caused by having a live cattle market at Smithfield were obvious, but the City of London, owners of the market and anxious to keep its privileges, was tardy in finding an alternative site outside the City. This led to the private venture of one John Perkins who, armed with an Act of Parliament, established in 1836 the Islington Cattle Market off Essex Road, near today's crescent numbered 246–294. The market was established in the teeth of, opposition from the City, the Smithfield butchers and other vested interests, but to the delight of those who were tired of the old regime. One newspaper in favour of the venture said that "The citizens will be deprived of the wholesome excitement occasioned by the sight of half-strangled oxen dying of thirst, the bellowing of bullocks, and yelling of drovers; the salubrious smells arising from the City cellar-hole slaughter-dens; and many other delights which the said citizens have hitherto enjoyed in full swing." Perkins hoped to cream off the trade coming and

going to the east but despite the provision of pens for 40,000 sheep, 7,000 cattle and 1,000 pigs, its convenience and its imposing buildings, it was not a success and quickly reverted to being lairs for cattle travelling to Smithfield. It left Mr Perkins with a loss of £100,000.

The City Corporation, however, could not for long put off its own responsibility in the matter and cast around for a site on which to relocate the live cattle market, leaving Smithfield to deal with carcasses. The Metropolitan Cattle Market, between York Way and Caledonian Road on the old Copenhagen Fields, was a spectacular affair. Opened in 1855, its build-

ings designed by J.B. Bunning, architect of some of the best public buildings of the day, it could, at any one time accommodate 7,000 cattle and 42,000 sheep. Space was also provided for calves and pigs, and ranged around the open market were offices for dealers, bankers, and railway and telegraph companies. Four new public houses on the perimeters were built and a handsome clock tower, now the centrepiece of the present dreary local authority housing, was erected. Market days were Mondays and Thursdays, and on Fridays miscellaneous animals such as horses, asses and goats were sold.

It is almost harder to imagine all these live beasts milling around built-up Islington than it is to envisage the open fields that preceded it. On other days a flea market took over the grounds, and a census in 1930 revealed that 2,100 stalls were there. All this came to an end in 1939.

104. *Flea Market at the Metropolitan Cattle Market*. A photograph taken between the wars.

105. *A view of Holloway Road, looking east.* From an engraving published in 1835. St John's church, built in 1828, may be seen in the distance.

The Heyday of Holloway Road

Unlikely as it seems now, Holloway Road, at least that stretch on either side of the Nags Head, was once a fashionable shopping centre. Its proliferation of shops, together with the tramway services, brought about a sharp decline in shopping centres as far away as Highgate Village, and stores like Jones Brothers made deliveries within a several-mile radius. This department store, begun as a small drapers by two Welsh brothers in 1867, had, by 1892, over 500 employees, 50 horses, 35 carts and vans, and in 1895 their printed catalogue ran to 1400 pages and over 3000 illustrations. Their emporium was an unfinished dream, as can be seen looking up at it from the outside. The dome was intended to be over the centre of the shop, but instead the sudden deterioration in the status of Holloway at the beginning of the 20th century put paid to plans to extend the store across the rest of the block.

Beale's, a restaurant and bakery which will be remembered by many readers for its atmosphere and *art deco* stained windows, was on the site of today's Sainsbury store. Thomas Beale also owned the Holloway Electrical Company in the days when electricity could be supplied by private companies, and

106. *Holloway Road at the turn of this century.*

he erected street lamps in the Holloway Road to light the trade.

A 1930s attempt to rejuvenate the area, the Holloway Arcade, was not a success and, like much of the area, stands derelict and neglected. As time goes by, and decisions about the area are delayed and delayed, the shopping trade goes elsewhere, perhaps irreversibly, and the multiples necessary for economic success will be difficult to entice back to a neighbourhood which deserves better bureaucracy.

107. *Beale's Restaurant, Holloway Road.* From a photograph of 1893.

108. *Holloway Road at the beginning of the 20th century.*

109. *The Northern Polytechnic.* From a postcard *c*1905.

ESTABLISHED 1848

MADAME HENRY,

SCIENTIFIC

Surgical Belt & Stay Maker.

STAYS & BELTS CUT
FOR DEFORMITIES.

RIDING, NURSING & SANITARY STAYS.

ONLY ADDRESS—

422, LIVERPOOL RD.,

HOLLOWAY, N.

Stays cut according to the human frame, giving protection to chest and abdomen and support to the back, by allowing the Stays to fall to the spine.

P.O.O. TO BE MADE PAYABLE TO CH. HENRY, 387, LIVERPOOL ROAD, N.

110. *Advertisement for Madame Henry, stay maker of Liverpool Road.*

Holloway Prison began as a gaol for the City of London. Originally the land was purchased in 1832 for use as a burial ground in the cholera epidemic that year, but this plan was never implemented. Twenty years later their architect, J.B. Bunning, who also designed the Metropolitan Cattle Market, built a fanciful prison instead, similar in some respects to Warwick Castle. In fact the public house opposite is called The Holloway Castle, the popular name for the prison. The original accommodation was for 283 men, 60 women and 60 juveniles, but since 1903, as a state prison, it has been used for women only. Oscar Wilde was imprisoned here in 1895 while on remand before his famous trial, and the detainment of suffragettes, including Sylvia and Emmeline Pankhurst, brought riots and a dynamite attack by sympathisers. The purpose of the architecture, of course, was to intimidate prisoners, and to emphasise the strength, longevity and security of the law. Its foundation stone bore the inscription 'May God preserve the City of London and make this place a terror to evil doers', and so it was unsurprising that the old building, whatever its architectural merits, was regarded as inappropriate for the modern treatment and rehabilitation of women prisoners. Demolition began in 1970.

111. *The New City Prison, Holloway.* An early illustration of Holloway Prison.

Holloway Prison

112. *Meeting discharged prisoners at the gates of Holloway Prison.*

113. *Michael Faraday.*

The Famous Names

Some notable residents or contributors to Islington life have already been mentioned. Others may be briefly noticed.

Charles Lamb, the writer, lived at No. 45 Chapel Street, and also at Colebrook Cottage, No. 64 Duncan Terrace; he was very happy here. Nearby, in recent times, Joe Orton, the playwright, lived and was murdered at No. 25 Noel Road. George Gissing, the writer, lived at No. 60 in the same road. Other writers included Thomas Hood, the poet, in a house on the site of No. 50 Essex Road, Mary Wollstonecraft, an early feminist, was in Cumming Street, off Pentonville Road, the poet Edmund Gosse was at No. 58 Huntingdon Street, and Tom Paine is alleged to have written *The Rights of Man* while staying at The Angel, although other claims exist for the birthplace of this famous work. Edward Lear, the humorist, was born in Holloway Road.

Canonbury Square was host to George Orwell at No. 27b, Evelyn Waugh and Nancy Mitford (though not at the same time) at No. 17a, while Duncan Grant lived with Vanessa Bell at No. 26a. Kate Greenaway, the children's writer, lived with her mother occasionally over a shop at No. 147 Upper Street.

An eccentric was Alexander Cruden, (1699–1770), who is commemorated by a plaque at No. 45 Camden Passage; not only did he compile a concordance to the Bible but, inflamed by the famous publication in 1763 of issue No. 45 of what was regarded by many as the seditious magazine *North Briton*, written by John Wilkes, he went round Islington erasing the number 45 wherever he found it. Two famous sportsmen lived in the Caledonian Road – Frederick Lilywhite, the cricketer, who kept a shop here, and the boxer Len Harvey who, on his retirement, kept the Star and Garter in Upper Street. The intrepid and famous balloonist, Charles Green, managed to live to a mature age and died at 51 Tufnell Park Road. Charles Cruft, the founder of the Dog Show, lived at No. 12 Highbury Grove, and his Show was held before the last War at the Royal Agricultural Hall. Dr. Crippen, whose relatively ordinary crime became famous for the nature of his flight and arrest, lived in Hilldrop Crescent; his house is now covered by Margaret Bondfield Court. Roger Fry lived in No. 7 Dalmeny Avenue, and Selwyn Image, the artist, round the corner at No. 78 Parkhurst Road.

Scientist Michael Faraday does not appear to have *lived* in Islington, but he was what was known as an 'Elder' at the Sandemanian Chapel in Bride Street, the site of which is now taken up by Faraday House, the telephone exchange. Sir Benjamin Britten the composer, and Sir Peter Pears the singer, lived at No. 8 Halliford Street. The late (Lord) Fenner Brockway MP, veteran pacifist, lived at No. 60 Myddelton Square, and prime minister Asquith was for a time in St. Mary's Grove.

114. *Highbury Corner*. This wide-angle photograph was probably taken before the 1st World War. To the left is the old Highbury Station and the Cock Tavern. Holloway Road is in the centre, and to the right is a large private house which is today's branch of Barclay's Bank.

The Coming of the Railways

Two major railways opened in Islington in 1850. In August, a temporary station in York Way served as the terminus for the extension to London of the Great Northern Railway, which connected it to Peterborough. This line, immediately north of the station, entered a 600-yard tunnel to go beneath the industrial premises south of Market Road and then, in a deep cutting emerged just west of Caledonian Road to cross Holloway Road and go north. With its associated goods yards it was sufficient to blight the whole area of Drayton Park, the vicinity becoming a wasteland as time went on and the railway contracted. At the time the line at this point went through open fields, but by the end of the century the whole rectangle of land, hemmed in by poorer housing, was covered with coal depots, gas works, electricity stations and the like.

The North London Railway, which opened to Islington a month later, caused blight of a different kind outside Islington. West of the parish the contours of the land demanded that it ran at rooftop level through the streets of Kentish and Camden Towns, thereby ruining the lives of many people whose win-

dows were yards from the track. In Islington, it ran across Caledonian Road and then went into a cutting, taking part of Arundel Square with it, and on to Canonbury and Hackney. The original name of this line was the East and West India Docks and Birmingham Junction Railway, which summed up, rather inelegantly, its function which was to convey freight between docks and Midlands: passenger traffic was an unexpected bonus. When its new terminus at Broad Street opened the railway company had by then realised the potential of City commuters, and this is reflected in the very imposing station it built in 1872 at Highbury Corner, shown in *Illustration 114*. London Transport has replaced this handsome building by what can only be described as an unfinished shed which lacks style, elegance and convenience.

In 1858 Newington Road and Balls Pond Station was opened on the same line; this was replaced by Canonbury Station in 1870.

The railway line which runs from Moorgate via Essex Road, Highbury and Drayton Park to Finsbury Park, has had an unusual number of owners. It was opened in 1904 by the Great Northern and City Railway, which, as its name implies, was an attempt by the Great Northern to coax commuters to the City via a change at Finsbury Park. In 1913 it was taken over by the Metropolitan Railway Company, whose line went through Moorgate, and its station at Highbury, still to be seen, is shown in *Illustration 119*. It was able to proclaim that from Highbury all parts of London could be reached, although there was, as there is now, an arduous change at Moorgate to achieve this. The London Passenger Transport Board took over in 1933 and then incorporated the line as an odd extension to the Northern line system, which was never very successful. In 1976 the whole stretch was reopened, more logically, as part of British Rail's electric service to the northern suburbs.

Meanwhile, the Great Northern, Piccadilly and Brompton Railway, today's Piccadilly underground line, opened in 1906 from Hammersmith to Finsbury Park. At that time there was a station in York Way – its red-tiled fascia is still to be seen. Lastly, the Victoria line was opened in 1968. It coincided with a general tendency to modernise, rather than destroy, older, architecturally attractive inner London areas, and more than any other factor contributed to the 'gentrification' of Islington.

Islington has long been an important stage in road

Highbury Station. (N. L. Ry.)

115. *Highbury Station on the North London line.* From a postcard *c*1905.

communications. Long distance coaches along the Great North Road to the City invariably stopped at Islington. Gradually, as more commuted, people living in inner London suburbs such as Islington and Holloway required short-run coaches to get to London. This trend was encouraged by local builders who, themselves, ran transport services to the City from places like Holloway.

The first tramway in Islington was opened in 1871 by the North Metropolitan Tramways Company, from the Nag's Head to Finsbury Square, via Upper Street and the Angel. Extensions to this were built to Archway and Finsbury Park the following year and it is interesting to note that these two destinations over the years became boundaries to the London transport system. This was particularly important to the Archway area, which became a turn-round for all sorts of routes and made the provision of a garage inevitable. The next few years saw further tramways to Ball's Pond, Camden Town, and King's Cross.

Motor buses replaced some trams by *c*1911 and trolleybuses took more of the old railed routes from 1938.

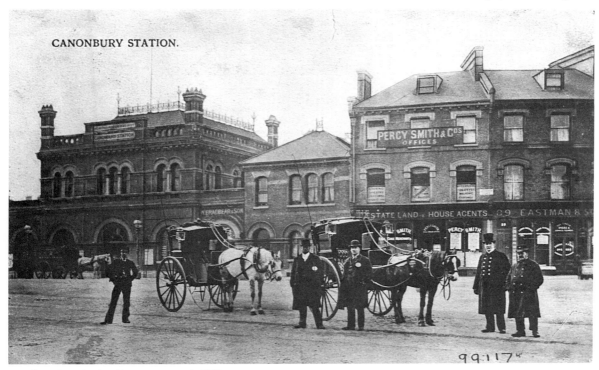

CANONBURY STATION.

116. *Canonbury Station.* From a postcard *c*1905.

117. *Highbury Railway Coal Depot.* This large depot was between Highbury Station and Crane Grove.

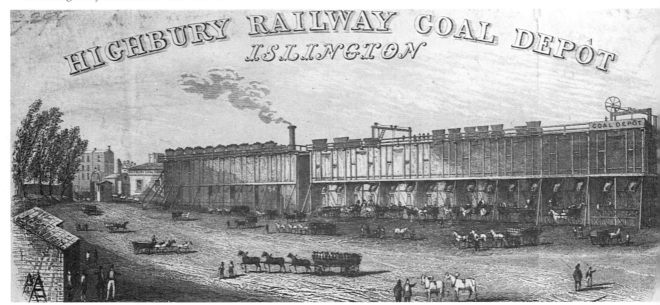

Facing page:
118. *Caledonian Road Station.* At the time of this postcard,
c1905, the entrance to the station was on the west side of
the road. At other times it has been in Roman Way, and
has recently been resited on the east side of Caledonian
Road.

Facing page:
119. *Highbury Underground Station.* At the time of this
photograph, c1933, the line was part of the Metropolitan
network.

Above:
120. *Holloway Bus Garage.*

Entertaining the People

121. *The interior of the Islington Literary and Scientific Institution, Almeida Street.*

Facing page:
122. *Today's Almeida Theatre, when used by the Salvation Army.*

During the mid-19th century Literary and Scientific Institutions sprung up throughout the country. Mostly they were middle-class affairs, although many had provision for attendance by people not able to afford the annual subscription. It was part of the Victorian view that knowledge, so long the province of an élite few, should be disseminated to a wider population, especially in view of the need to administrate and educate a growing working-class and an empire. In institutions everywhere lectures on cultural subjects and the new discoveries of science took place, and in their way these places became the *cultural* hub of the community, a role not satisfactorily assumed by the Church which, in any case,

was not in tune with scientific advancement and the new theories of evolution and creation. This middle-class movement was copied by the Working Men's Clubs, doing the same sort of thing for a different social class, and from these came a call for free libraries and free education for all.

The institutions themselves were rarely innovatory in social terms: political discussion was frowned upon and discouraged, but they represented a new order of local influence, away from the old landholders and the disputatious vestrymen with vested interests.

LONDON. AGRICULTURAL HALL.

Facing page:
123. *The Royal Agricultural Hall, Islington.* From a postcard
*c*1905.

Facing page:
124. *The Liverpool Road entrance to the Royal Agricultural Hall.*
From a postcard.

Only one such institution survives in London now
– in Highgate Village, and by a quirk of fortune,
probably more prosperous now than it has ever
been. In the rest of the country few exist, and even
these were probably kept alive not so much by the
membership, but by the patronage of a bequest from
a local industrialist.

The Islington Literary and Scientific Institution
was formed in 1832, and in a building designed by
Gough and Roumieu in what is now Almeida Street,
met from 1838. It fell upon hard times towards the
end of the century and by 1890 the Salvation Army
had taken the place, where it remained until 1952. It
was then used as a warehouse by Beck's Carnival
Novelties and looked as though it might go the way
of many handsome buildings, but it has been rescued
by the Almeida Theatre and generous grant-giving
bodies to be, not only a fine theatre, but a striking
example of the work of its architects.

The Smithfield Club held annual livestock shows
from 1798; these outgrew their premises and it was
probably no accident that the site of some cattle lairs
at Islington, on the road to Smithfield and a place
familiar to everyone connected with livestock, was
chosen for their new Agricultural Hall. The first part
was built in 1862 to the designs of Frederick Peck,
using a cast-iron and glass roof giving a 125ft span.

125. *The Holloway Empire, Holloway Road.* From a postcard
*c*1905.

126. *The Grand Theatre, Islington High Street.* From a postcard *c*1905.

Facing page:
127. *The Carlton Cinema, Essex Road, just before it opened in 1930.*

Enlargements occurred over the years so that it might be used for a variety of functions. It featured recitals, dog shows, circuses, marathons and cycle races, and one hall became a cinema, eventually the Gaumont, which closed in 1963. The remainder of the Hall was requisitioned in the last war for use as a sorting office and so it continued until 1971 when it was vacated. It seemed, after that, destined for demolition. It did not have a great many vociferous or influential supporters, it stood in the way of a possible road scheme which might solve Islington's traffic problem at the Angel and, furthermore, the building had suffered during its time as a sorting office. It took some persistence on the part of conservationists to save the building. They were helped, one feels, by the delays which always attend such matters, so that by the time the question was considered really seriously developers and planning authorities had an appetite for theme parks and exhibition halls. In the event the persistence of Mr. Sam Morris, whose dedication to the project ensured that conversion of this splendid building was sympathetically done, brought about today's Business Design Centre.

Islington has been well supplied with theatres and cinemas. In Holloway Road alone there there three theatres in that road's heyday. The Parkhurst at No. 401 was built in 1890, originally as a hall and then as a full-blown theatre eight years later. It had a short life, became a cinema in 1909 and was demolished *c*1930; the derelict Holloway Arcade is on its site. The Holloway Empire, at No. 564, was opened in 1899; it was built by one of the two most prolific theatre architects of the day, W.G.R. Sprague. By 1924, with the thirst for variety and music-hall abated, it became a cinema and was eventually closed in 1953. Offices are now on the site. The third theatre was the Marlborough. This was built by the other theatre architect of the day, Frank Matcham, in 1903 at No. 383 Holloway Road. It, too, became a cinema, was demolished in 1962 and the Marlborough building of the Polytechnic of North London is on its site.

In central Islington the two principal theatres were the Grand Theatre (later called the Islington Empire), and Collin's Music Hall. Fire was the enemy of the Grand during most of its existence. It began as a concert hall in 1860, was burnt down first in 1882,

and was rebuilt by Frank Matcham in 1883; this lasted four years before another fire destroyed it; it was rebuilt the next year by Frank Matcham again, with a capacity of 3,000. This, too, was burnt down, in 1900. Frank Matcham, no doubt by this time familiar with the site, rebuilt it again in 1901, but it became a cinema in 1939. It closed in 1962 and the facade lingered on until 1982.

Collin's Music Hall was on the site of the timber yard by Islington Green. Throughout its career it rarely had pretensions to be a theatre and was usually a music hall from its opening in 1862 until its closure in 1958, when a fire destroyed much of the building. It derived its name from the licensee in 1863, who was called Samuel Collins Vagg. Many famous variety artists appeared here, including Tommy Trinder, George Robey, Fred Karno, Marie Lloyd, Harry Lauder and Albert Chevalier.

Some Islington cinemas were converted theatres but the most spectacular were purpose-built. The Carlton, in Essex Road, was built in 1930, in the neo-Egyptian style of the time and with a sumptuous

Below:
128. *The interior of the Carlton Cinema, Essex Road.*

Facing page:
129. *The Electric Cinema in Upper Street, now Dome Antiques.*

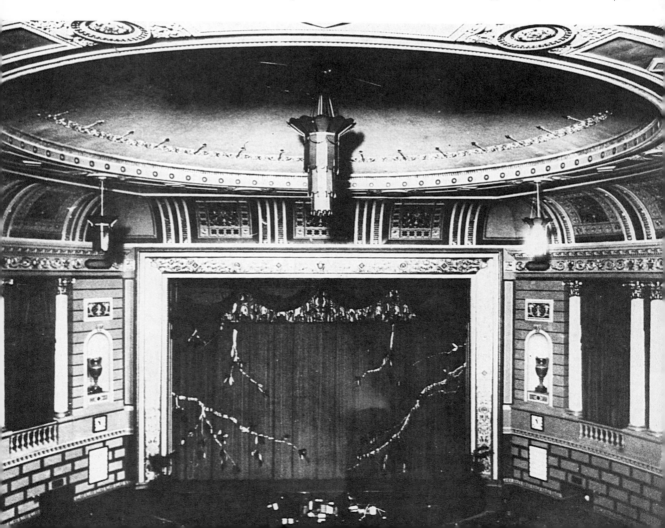

Above:
130. *The Coronet Cinema, Essex Road.*

Below:
131. *The Cinematograph Theatre, Seven Sisters Road, Finsbury Park.*

132. *St. George's church, Tufnell Park.* This building is now used as a theatre.

interior. (See *Illustrations 127 and 128*). Also in Essex Road, on the corner with Packington Street, was the Coronet. Built in 1912, this was one of the earlier specially-built cinemas at a time when many were converted theatres. Another early cinema was the Electric at No. 75 Upper Street, which is now occupied by Dome Antiques. Happily, its striking frontage survives. Nearby, the Screen-on-the-Green is an unlikely survivor from the cinema age. It opened in 1911, very much on the cheap, as the Picture Theatre, and went through various unsuccessful lives until, in the 1970s, it became the Screen-on-the-Green and, much against the trend of that era, flourished.

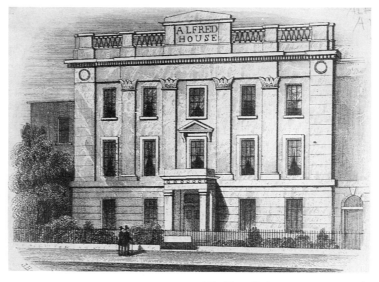

133. *The Alfred House Collegiate School.*

School Days

134. *Islington Proprietary School, Barnsbury Street.* From an engraving published in 1835.

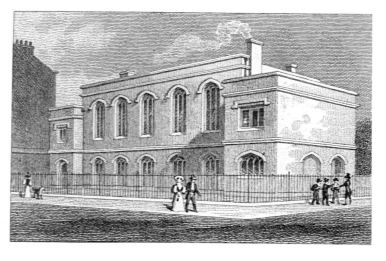

135. *The Priory Pestalozzian School for the Middle Classes.* This school was established in 1848.

Until the Education Act of 1870 established free primary schools education was, even for those able to afford it, hazardous. There were what became known as 'Dame Schools', really establishments run by one or more maiden or widowed ladies trying to supplement a fixed income. The standard of education, especially as women themselves received little, could not have been good. Other schools rejoiced in the title of 'Academy'. Here, perhaps, was the stuff of Dickens, of sadistic masters, of neglected, miserable, rough-fighting boys. Here were students of all abilities forced to apply themselves to subjects, such as Greek, beyond their capabilities or interest. There were charity schools, usually the remnant of establishments set up in the 17th or 18th centuries, where the master might well be the local curate or priest, who, perhaps, saw his function at the school as to instil nothing more than the three Rs and a good dose of religion. Other charity schools dealt with the really poor. These were called Ragged Schools and here the battle was to persuade parents to part with the labour of their children so that they could learn some elementary skills. At the other end of the scale the affluent would send their male children to residential grammar schools and obtain a governess for their daughters.

For much of the 19th century the majority of children were educated in 'British' or 'National' schools. British Schools began in 1808 using a system developed by Joseph Lancaster by which the taught pupils themselves soon became instructors of the younger ones, under the supervision of the paid staff. This was economic and meant, too, that large numbers of children could be handled. By 1851, there were 1500 such schools in the country.

The main rival to these schools, which were organised by the British and Foreign School Society, were those begun, three years later, by the National Society for the Education of the Poor in the Principles of the Established Church. Here, the facilities of the churches were at the disposal of the Society. Church halls could be used, and the influence of the vicar and his colleagues could be brought to bear, so that children were educated by the National Society rather than by the British schools, which mainly drew their support from nonconformist parents. By 1851 there were 17,000 National schools.

Various types of schools are shown in *Illustrations 133–139.* The Alfred House Collegiate Institute for Young Ladies, location unknown, was run by a Trevillian Spicer from 1849, with the intention of proving that 'the intellectual capabilities of women were equal to those of men'. The Islington Proprietary School, later the Islington High School, was founded

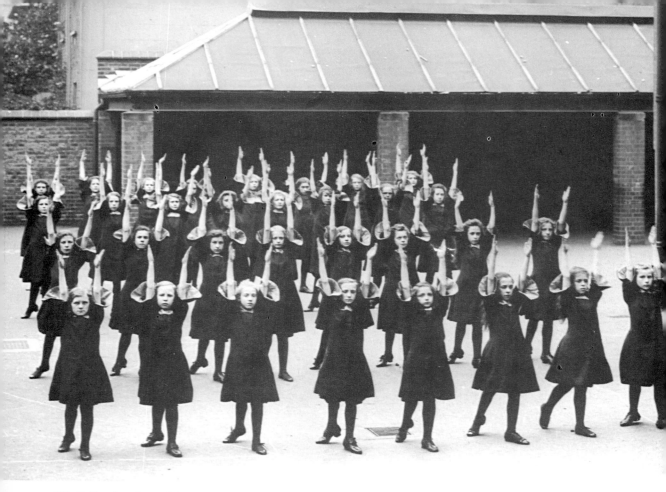

136. *Drill at Copenhagen Primary School, 1906.*

in 1830. The building shown in *Illustration 134* was in Barnsbury Street, near to Milner Square. The 'proprietors' were professional people, local traders being excluded; each proprietor could nominate one free pupil for each share held in the venture, and the rule was that the headmaster should be an Anglican clergyman. This school continued until 1897, when the building became a syphon factory and then a manufactory for greeting cards. It has recently been demolished and apartments built on the site.

Illustration 135 shows the 'Priory Pestalozzian School, Islington, for the Middle Classes', which was established in 1848. There was no reticence in those days in stating the social class of pupil to be catered for – Middle Class Schools were common. However, a school run on the principles evolved by Johann Pestalozzi, a Swiss educational reformer, and in which children learnt by experience rather than by rote, was a rarer item.

137. *Remedial treatment at Highbury Truant School.*

The 1870 Education Act established a system of elementary Board schools; each was, in theory, secular and undenominational. They attracted considerable opposition – from ratepayers who resented their cost, from religious bodies who objected to competition to their own schools, from charities who saw their work done for them, and from parents hostile to education in the first place. It is probable that a number of parents connived at their children's non-attendance. At any rate, the problem was sufficient for special area schools for truants to be set up, such as the one in Highbury, shown in *Illustration 137*.

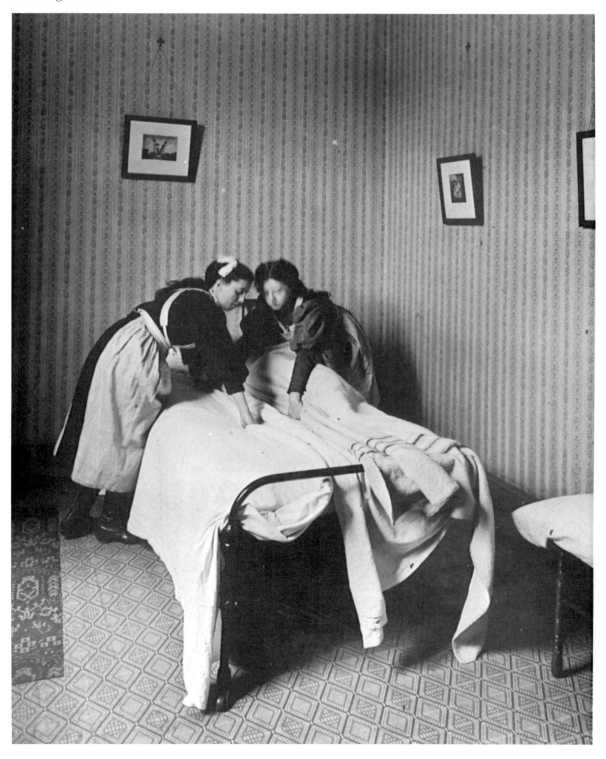

Facing page:
138. *Domestic Science lesson at Barnsbury Park School, 1908.*

Above:
139. *Caledonian Road Board School.*

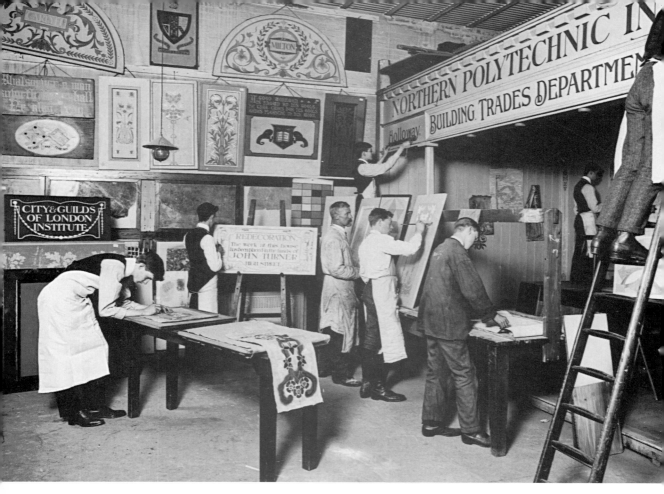

140. *The Building Trades' Workshop at the Northern Polytechnic, Holloway Road.*

141. *Advertisement for the Northern Polytechnic, 1909.*

The Northern Polytechnic in Holloway Road was opened in 1896 in a building designed by Charles Bell; a large hall, later the theatre, opened the following year. Its main emphasis then was on skilled trades, as *Illustration 141* shows. The Polytechnic has expanded greatly since then and has other buildings, including a substantial annexe in Kentish Town, and a modern tower block, arguably the ugliest building in Islington, in Holloway Road.

NORTHERN POLYTECHNIC INSTITUTE,

HOLLOWAY,

Close to the New G.N. & Piccadilly Tube, to the Holloway Station, G.N.R., and five minutes' walk from Highbury Station, N.L.R., and Drayton Park Station, G.N. and City Railway.

Engineering Day School,
Fees £15 per Annum.

Building Day School,
Fees £10 10s. per Annum.

ENGINEERING & ARCHITECTS' APPRENTICES

CAN ALSO ATTEND PART-TIME COURSES.

FEES BY ARRANGEMENT.

TRAINING SCHOOL FOR DOMESTIC ECONOMY TEACHERS.

Cookery, Laundry, Dressmaking & Needlework.

FEES £8 per Term.

AN APPRENTICESHIP SCHOOL

In which Boys can obtain their Earlier Training as Carpenters or Plumbers.

The Traders

It is one of the surprises of looking through old street directories to compare the trades advertised to those of today. Holloway Road is an example. Looking at 1913 we find a *Mrs* Miles who was a chimney cleaner, a perambulator manufacturer, a blind manufacturer, a shoeing forge, a saddler, a bust maker, a bird fancier, a ham and beef warehouse, a brush maker, a ladder maker, an artificial teeth maker, tennis racket makers and so on.

Some trades had an importance then which has entirely disappeared. For example, Ridley's imposing floor cloth factory in Essex Road had its counterpart near Brecknock Road, where another large building, depicted by Shepherd, existed. Breweries are a classic example of the centralisation of manufacture. At the turn of this century probably every town had at least one brewery which supplied many of the public houses in the vicinity. Gordon's Caledonian Road brewery, depicted in *Illustration 147*, competed against others in Brewery Road and Holloway Road, and had an extensive network of deliveries.

142. *Samuel Ridley's Floor Cloth Factory, Essex Road.*

Above:
143. *Entrance to the brewery in Brewery Road.*

Below:
144. *The Highbury Pantechnicon Company.*

145. *Advertisement for Penfold's the printers of Islington, 1909.*

146. *Advertisement in 1909 for George Morris & Co, shirtmakers of 17 Islington High Street.*

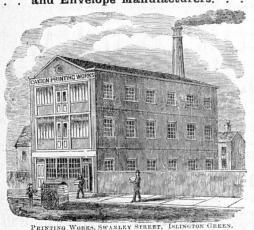

PENFOLD & SONS,

Newspaper, Magazine, Book, and General Printing Contractors, .

Wholesale and Retail Stationers, .

Bookbinders, Account Book Makers,

. . and Envelope Manufacturers. . .

PRINTING WORKS, SWANLEY STREET, ISLINGTON GREEN.

Penfold's .
Perfect . .
END FOR . .   *Printing .*
. ESTIMATES.   *Pleases . .*
Particular
People. . .

HEAD OFFICE,
STATIONERY WAREHOUSE
AND BOOKBINDING DEPT. } **353a, Upper St., Islington.**

SPECIALITY IN SHIRTS.
GEO. MORRIS & CO.,
Having had over 45 years' experience as
Shirt Makers and Fitters,
And holding as they do over
5,000 SHIRT PATTERNS
(A special one cut for every customer for future reference), may fairly claim a reputation scarcely equalled by any firm of the same trade in London.
We hold some Hundreds of Testimonials, from all parts of the country and abroad, testifying to the excellence of our Shirts, both for Fit and Wear.
N.B.—A Sample Shirt will have same attention as an order for a dozen. Perfect fit guaranteed.

CASH——
——SYSTEM.

Flannel Shirts,
From **3/6.**

Tunic Shirts,
From **2/6.**

New Plaited Dress Shirts,
3/6.

Established 1862.

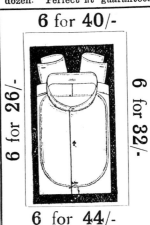

CASH——
——SYSTEM.

Motor Wraps,
RUGS,
Dressing Gowns,
BAGS,
Ladies' and
Gentlemen's
UMBRELLAS.

Established 1862.

THE BEST HALF-CROWN GLOVE IN LONDON.
For Ladies or Gentlemen.

MORLEY'S NATURAL LLAMA & SCOTCH WOOL UNDERCLOTHING.
A LARGE STOCK to select from, at LOWEST PRICES.
Dr. Jaeger's Sanitary Wool Underclothing.

17, HIGH ST., ISLINGTON
(NINE DOORS FROM "ANGEL," SAME SIDE.)

A. GORDON & Co.

Caledonian   Road

CALEDONIAN BREWERY.

99427"

ALE AND PORTER BREWERS.   London.

Beg to inform their Friends and Customers, that in consequence of the removal of the extra War Tax imposed on Malt in May 1854, the prices of Pale & Mild Ales, Stout and Porter are reduced as follows.

LIST OF PRICES IN BOTTLES.
is subjoined, to which attention is respectfully solicited

	IN BOTTLES - PER DOZEN.		
	Quarts.	Pints.	Imp.ᵗ Pints.
Fine Tonic Ale, Bitter	3ˢ 3ᵈ	2ˢ 0ᵈ	2ˢ 9ᵈ
Superior do do	4 . 3	2 . 6	3 . 3
India Pale Ale	4 . 9	2 . 9	3 . 9
Strong Ale, full body & Fine Scotch flavor	5 . 6	3 . 3	4 . 3
Fine Porter	3 . 9	2 . 3	3 . 0
Superior Single Stout	4 . 3	2 . 6	3 . 3
Extra Double Stout	4 . 9	2 . 9	3 . 9

Bottles Charged, and allowed for when returned, but if not returned they must be paid for on Delivery.

TERMS CASH ON DELIVERY SUBJECT TO A DISCOUNT OF 3ᵈ PER DOZEN.
The Discount will not be allowed unless paid on delivery.

THE DRAYS DELIVER AS UNDER.

Monday.	Tuesday.	Wednesday.	Thursday.	Friday.	Saturday.
Kentish Town Haverstock hill and Hampstead Walworth Camberwell and Peckham Stoke Newington Hackney and Clapton	Oxford Street to New Road Edgeware Rᵈ Bayswater & Notting Hill Clerkenwell City & Wapping Bermondsey Rotherhithe Deptford & Greenwich	Stepney Limehouse Poplar and Millwall Lambeth Brixton & Clapham Holloway Hornsey & Tottenham	Kentish Town Regents Park & St Johns Wood Mile End Bow & Bromley Canonbury Lower Road & Kingsland	Strand Westminster & Chelsea Clerkenwell City and Wapping Rotherhithe Deptford & Greenwich	Bloomsbury Holborn and Chancery Lane Stepney, Poplar Limehouse & Millwall Holloway Highgate Finchley

* ISLINGTON DAILY.

Families are respectfully requested to observe that all orders should be sent at least one day previous to delivery.

COUNTRY ORDERS (ENCLOSING A REMITTANCE IN FULL) PUNCTUALLY ATTENDED TO.

The Cheapest and Best Establishment in the Metropolis for all classes of Funerals.

Funerals conducted on a Reform Principle with Superior and Modern Equipments.   Superior Class of Horses.
Open or Closed Hearses, Cars and Modern Broughams.

W. J. RIDER

(Late W. E. SHARMAN),

General Funeral Furnisher & Undertaker,

390, CALEDONIAN ROAD, N., close to N.L.R. Station.

Facing page:
147. *Advertisement for A. Gordon's Caledonian Road Brewery, 1857.*

Above:
148. *Advertisement for W.J. Rider, undertaker of Caledonian Road, 1909.*

Below:
149. *Chapel Market.* From a postcard posted in 1915.

150. *Barossa Lodge, formerly at 296–300 Essex Road.* A photograph taken in the late 1930s.

151. *Archway Road, 1955.* The striking lack of traffic just over thirty years ago is shown.

152. *Camden Passage, 1954.* The Passage when it was a general shopping centre and before the antique shops took over.

Post-war Years

The nature of central Islington has changed in the past twenty years. Incomers who were once derided for their 'gentrification' of the area, are themselves quick to pour scorn on the new 'yuppies' whose activities have made the area even more expensive to buy into. There is now a clear demarcation between those who live in well-groomed terraces and squares and those who live in local authority estates, many of which are run-down and badly maintained. This transformation has aroused strong passions, especially in those on the one hand who feel dispossesed of their own, and their parents' neighbourhoods, and those on the other who have rescued derelict properties left in bad repair from the effects of rent control legislation, and who have poured their energies and incomes into renovation. The interests of these two parties will probably never coincide and

Above:
153. *Derelict houses in Canonbury Square in the 1950s.*

Below:
154. *Bewdley Street, Barnsbury in 1967, before 'gentrification'.*

Facing page:
155. *The headquarters of Repuke, undertakers of St Peter's Street. It is said that this company was the last in north London to continue providing horses and carriages for funerals.*

156. *A run – down Gibson Square in 1938.*

those passions will not be appeased.

The debate is part of a much larger, and fascinating, phenomenon which will keep social historians of the future very occupied. There is now, for example, an unparalleled emphasis in English society through all classes, on care for the home. Without doubt, most areas of Islington are probably in their best state since they were built. Or, it may often be observed, the very people who are buying and transforming old properties, middle-class by income, are quite often of recent working-class origins. They are returning to areas gratefully forsaken by a previous generation of tenants who despaired of damp, lack of bathrooms and general seediness, and who moved to local authority or new-town housing elsewhere.

It is possible, walking round Islington, to forget just how seedy it looked in the past. In this section are photographs of a number of buildings in what are now regarded as prime streets, showing the degree of dereliction which prevailed. Far worse properties existed and many of these were torn down without thought of renovation by local authorities in the Utopian decades after the last war, although in Islington the destruction of old terraces,has been less than in some other boroughs. Somehow, most of the very attractive terraces and squares have survived but it is unlikely that they would have done without the massive injection of private money and *day-to-day* care which has come with private ownership. It is inconceivable that the local authorities would have had the money, the resources or, it has to be said, the professional imagination, to have dealt with so vast a prob-

157. *The junction of Essex Road and Islington Green, c1910.*

lem. In the 1960s, before the conservation movement had gathered momentum and when it was comparatively easy for local authorities to take over and comprehensively demolish whole areas of old housing, the professional way forward for housing was for inward-looking estates whose architectural pretensions, or lack of them, are now the source of much, and quite justifiable, discontent. Islington has escaped the worst of that period of planning and architecture.

Housing estates aside, the only sensible way to integrate classes of people in the terraces of Islington was the policy of the Council to buy individual houses and to rent them out: this at least, (or it was before the prices of houses outstripped the local authority budget), was a way of facing up to the inexorable march of market forces. But even this small piece of social engineering is now to be eroded as tenants are encourged to buy and sell such properties.

158. *No. 61 Cross Street in 1945.*

159. No. 185 Barnsbury Road in 1945.

Index